THE FOOD AND COOKING OF
POLAND

THE FOOD AND COOKING OF
POLAND

TRADITIONS • INGREDIENTS • TASTES • TECHNIQUES • OVER 60 CLASSIC RECIPES

EWA MICHALIK

with photographs by Jon Whitaker

aquamarine

This edition is published by Aquamarine, an imprint of Anness Publishing Ltd,
Hermes House,
88–89 Blackfriars Road,
London SE1 8HA
tel. 020 7401 2077
fax 020 7633 9499

www.aquamarinebooks.com
www.annesspublishing.com

If you like the images in this book and would like to investigate using them for publishing, promotions or advertising, please visit our website www.practicalpictures.com for more information.

UK agent: The Manning Partnership Ltd;
tel. 01225 478444; fax 01225 478440;
sales@manning-partnership.co.uk

UK distributor: Grantham Book Services Ltd;
tel. 01476 541080; fax 01476 541061;
orders@gbs.tbs-ltd.co.uk

North American agent/distributor:
National Book Network; tel. 301 459 3366;
fax 301 429 5746; www.nbnbooks.com

Australian agent/distributor:
Pan Macmillan Australia;
tel. 1300 135 113; fax 1300 135 103
customer.service@macmillan.com.au

New Zealand agent/distributor:
David Bateman Ltd; tel. (09) 415 7664
fax (09) 415 8892

Publisher: Joanna Lorenz
Senior Managing Editor: Conor Kilgallon
Project Editor: Lucy Doncaster
Contributing Editor: Catherine Best
Designer: Sarah Rock
Illustrator: Rob Highton
Photography: Jon Whitaker
Food Stylists: Claire Ptak and Joy Skipper
Prop Stylist: Penny Markham
Production Controller: Mai-Ling Collyer

Ethical Trading Policy

At Anness Publishing we believe that business should be conducted in an ethical and ecologically sustainable way, with respect for the environment and a proper regard to the replacement of the natural resources we employ.

As a publisher, we use a lot of wood pulp to make high-quality paper for printing, and that wood commonly comes from spruce trees. We are therefore currently growing more than 500,000 trees in two Scottish forest plantations near Aberdeen – Berrymoss (130 hectares/320 acres) and West Touxhill (125 hectares/305 acres). The forests we manage contain twice the number of trees employed each year in paper-making for our books.

Because of this ongoing ecological investment programme, you, as our customer, can have the pleasure and reassurance of knowing that a tree is being cultivated on your behalf to naturally replace the materials used to make the book you are holding.

Our forestry programme is run in accordance with the UK Woodland Assurance Scheme (UKWAS) and will be certified by the internationally recognized Forest Stewardship Council (FSC). The FSC is a non-government organization dedicated to promoting responsible management of the world's forests. Certification ensures forests are managed in an environmentally sustainable and socially responsible basis. For further information about this scheme, go to www.annesspublishing.com/trees

Notes

Bracketed terms are intended for American readers.

For all recipes, quantities are given in both metric and imperial measures and, where appropriate, in standard cups and spoons. Follow one set of measures, but not a mixture, because they are not interchangeable.

Standard spoon and cup measures are level. 1 tsp = 5ml, 1 tbsp = 15ml, 1 cup = 250ml/8fl oz.

Australian standard tablespoons are 20ml. Australian readers should use 3 tsp in place of 1 tbsp for measuring small quantities of gelatine, flour, salt, etc.

American pints are 16fl oz/2 cups. American readers should use 20fl oz/2.5 cups in place of 1 pint when measuring liquids.

Electric oven temperatures in this book are for conventional ovens. When using a fan oven, the temperature will probably need to be reduced by about 10–20°C/20–40°F. Since ovens vary, you should check with your manufacturer's instruction book for guidance.

The nutritional analysis given for each recipe is calculated per portion (i.e. serving or item), unless otherwise stated. If the recipe gives a range, such as Serves 4–6, then the nutritional analysis will be for the smaller portion size, i.e. 6 servings. Measurements for sodium do not include salt added to taste.

Medium (US large) eggs are used unless otherwise stated.

The very young, the elderly, pregnant women and those in ill-health or with a compromised immune system are advised against eating dishes containing raw eggs.

Front cover shows Breaded Pork Cutlets (see page 72).

Contents

Poland: the land and its history

Surrounded on most of its borders by powerful neighbouring countries, Poland was for centuries subjected to repression and occupation by other nations. And no wonder, for this was a prize worth capturing; in addition to its strategic geographical position, the fertile countryside abounds with all manner of good things to eat – from vast fields of grain and lakes and rivers teeming with freshwater fish, to large forests inhabited by all kinds of animals and birds suitable for the table. This diverse wealth of local ingredients, coupled with the techniques and ingredients brought by invading countries, gave rise to the rich and unique culinary tradition that is known and loved all over the world today.

The geography of the country

Poland's shape – a square with the south-western corner chewed away – is dominated by the natural boundaries of the Baltic Sea to the north and the Sudeten, Tatra and Carpathian mountain ranges to the south. On its western and eastern borders, however, there are no such physical delineations. On the western border the only sign that you are passing from Germany to Poland is the Oder river, which wends its way from south to north towards the sea. On the eastern side, not even a river valley separates Poland from its neighbours, the Russian enclave Kaliningrad, Lithuania, Belarus and Ukraine.

This lack of natural boundaries has proved inviting to Poland's neighbours, who have, in the past, been tempted to take advantage of Poland's abundant natural resources for their own use.

However, Poland's position as a kind of pivot nestling between Western and Eastern Europe, as well as between the warm south and the chilly north, also has its advantages, including exposure to many different cultures and their corresponding trading links. As a result, the Poles have been able to adapt their cuisine to use a mixture of local ingredients and imported crops, such as potatoes and salad vegetables, which now flourish in the fertile soil.

A good farming climate

Temperatures and growing conditions in Poland vary only slightly from one side of the country to the other, with warmer, wetter weather in the south-west and colder, drier areas in the north-east. The whole country can be very cold in the winter as the biting north-westerly winds sweep across mainland Europe and Scandinavia, picking up rain and snow clouds from the Baltic. Summer temperatures are rather more variable, depending on the prevailing air currents, although the reliable gentle summer rains bring stable growing conditions for the crops of central Poland and ensure that there is always enough summer pasture for the cattle and food for the pigs.

To make the most of such fertile conditions the people of Poland have developed many ways of working with the climate to maximize crop yields from the land. They also knew how to make sure there was enough food to see them through the lean times of year, and this led to many excellent, tasty recipes based on meat, game, root vegetables, grains and freshwater fish, combined with preserved foods such as sauerkraut, curd cheese, sour cream and, of course, the famously strong and flavoursome local vodka.

LEFT The rolling arable fields in central Poland are ideally suited to the climate.

Northern lakes

The region in northern Poland that borders the Baltic Sea is a flat wetland dominated by waterways and home to many of the country's 10,000 lakes. These lakes are teeming with a great variety of freshwater fish, a fantastic source of protein that has been part of Polish cuisine since the earliest days. Pike, carp and trout in particular grow to a good size, and are served to the whole family on feast days such as Christmas, where carp is set in jelly or simmered in a wine stock. In the past it was traditional to keep the carp alive until the last possible moment before it was cooked to ensure its freshness – often even swimming in the family's bathtub!

The Baltic coastline is smooth, with the strong currents of the Baltic driving shoals of fish past Poland and on to the Baltic states and Scandinavia. Poland's relatively short sea border ends with a swirl at Gdansk, where the Vistula river meets the sea and a long spit of silt from the river has formed a natural lagoon. Fishing fleets based on the coast catch sardines, haddock, lobster and other seafood, but over-fishing and pollution in the Baltic means that many have to travel much longer distances to find enough fish.

RIGHT Bordered by seven different countries, Poland is open to many cultural influences.

In this spongy northern terrain, some of which is below sea level, there is little room between the lakes and forests for large-scale agriculture. Farms tend to be very small family affairs, with just a few pigs and cattle and the growing of root crops, particularly potatoes – a staple of many Polish dishes, including pancakes and dumplings.

Central plains

Like the northern lake region, the central part of Poland is also very flat, but less liberally sprinkled with lakes. This gives the farmers more room to grow cereals and to keep cattle, although family farms tend to be rather

ABOVE LEFT The stunning Baltic coastline is home to many different types of fish. ABOVE Carp, a favourite on the Polish table at Christmas, are found in the many lakes.

small and many still produce only enough food for their owners, rather than trading on a larger scale.

Shaped by the glaciers of the Ice Age, this flat landscape is rich in natural resources, particularly coal, and this led to considerable industrialization during the 19th and 20th centuries. Today, the industries have moved elsewhere, leaving a legacy of pollution, run-down housing and a lack of jobs for the local people.

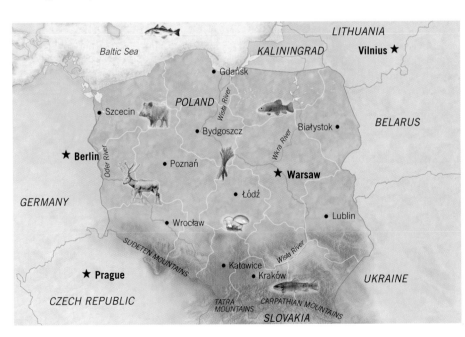

City life

The capital city, Warsaw, like many of the other major cities of Poland, is situated in the central region of Poland. Now that the restrictions of earlier years have been lifted there is a flourishing restaurant trade in these cities, and people love to go out on special occasions to eat their favourite foods – dumplings (pierogi) filled with savoury or sweet mixtures, filling soups, hunter's stew (bigos) and the delectable cakes and pastries made by the many bakers to be found in the towns and cities.

Southern mountains

To the south, Poland's natural border is formed by the spectacular mountain ranges that divide the country from the Czech Republic and Slovakia. With most of Poland's hills rarely rising to more than 300m/1,000ft above sea level, the contrast between the plains and the southern fringe is extreme. The highest mountain, Mount Rysy, in the Tatra range on the border with Slovakia, is 2,499m/8,200ft above sea level, while the lowest point, located west of the village of Raczki Elbląskie, is 1.8m/5.9ft below sea level.

The foothills to these mountains support a range of animals, including sheep, pigs and cattle. Hay fields rising

RIGHT Hay is used to feed the cattle, sheep and pigs that graze on the foothills.

gently up the slopes are a common sight and are cultivated in order to feed the animals. Despite the abundance of sheep, lamb is not a favourite meat in Poland – they are more often kept for their wool, to be made into clothing ready for the cold winters, and their milk, to be made into a much-loved sharp-tasting sheep's cheese.

Despite the winter cold, the region is well-populated, with family farms predominating. Some entrepreneurial inhabitants now take advantage of their position in the fresh mountain air to encourage tourists to stay for walking holidays, fortified by hearty stews and maybe the fierce local plum brandy (Śliwowica Łacka). Other local industries include food processing plants, which now package the abundant meat, dairy and food crops of the region to be sent all over Poland and further afield.

ABOVE The beautiful Tatra mountain range forms a natural border with Slovakia.

The first Polish kingdom

Prior to 966, the year of the earliest recorded historical event and first written reference to a Polish state, the region now known as Poland was inhabited by various tribes, including the Polanie, Wislanie, Pomorzanie and Mazovians. With the baptism of Mieszko I, duke of the Slavic tribe of Polans, in 966, the tribes, known collectively as the West Slavs, were united, and within 25 years had become one of the most powerful states in eastern Europe.

For the next 800 years Poland was a flourishing sovereign state, which made trading and cultural links with other countries through a combination of adventurous exploration and royal

marriages. In addition, from 1569–1791 Poland joined with Lithuania to form a commonwealth that was beneficial to both countries and made them a strong force in Eastern Europe.

With hunting parties providing venison, hare, pheasant and duck from the woods; mushrooms and herbs growing abundantly in the deep forests; and fish filling the lakes, ready to be fried, simmered, or made into soup, medieval Poland already had a strong and diverse culinary culture. With the formation of strong links with the rest of Europe, however, cooking techniques and ingredients from western and southern Europe, especially France and Italy, started to have a huge influence on Polish food. In addition, spices from the East started to be incorporated, being used, in particular, to disguise the flavour of any meat or game that was perhaps past its best.

With the arrival in 1518 of an Italian princess, Queen Bona Sforza, to marry King Sigismund I, Polish cooking began to evolve into the rich cuisine of today. Homesick for Italy, she encouraged French and Italian cooks to visit Poland, bringing with them more delicate recipes for soups and stews as well as new ingredients, including cabbage, leeks, lettuce and celeriac, which were adopted with enthusiasm.

Division of the spoils

From the end of the 18th century until the end of the 20th century, the history of Poland has been one of occupation and turmoil. For many years the land was controlled by different powers, including Russia, Prussia and Austria. This was followed by a brief period of independence from 1918–39, which ended abruptly when Nazi Germany invaded in 1939. After the war the country fell under Communist rule and the domination of the USSR until 1989.

Over 20 per cent of the population of Poland died during World War II, most of them Jews and other ethnic minorities who were transported to concentration camps. Resourceful survivors had their natural food stocks to fall back on when imports became scarce, but even these were often taken from them in the later 20th century to feed other mouths, or wasted under the centralized Communist system. Despite an attempt to establish collective farms under this system after 1945, however, the traditional Polish system of small-scale agriculture somehow survived, along with many closely guarded age-old local recipes and ingredients.

The 21st century

Poland has changed radically since the uprising against the Communist leaders in the 1980s, which was led by Lech Wałęsa and the Solidarity trade union based in the Gdansk shipyards. It now has its own democratic government, although several Communist party members have been returned to power now that the people are free to choose their own representatives. It has also joined NATO and the EU, and a free flow of goods and people passes once again into and out of the country.

As with many fast-changing countries, a large number of Polish workers go abroad to further their careers in more prosperous parts of the world. And wherever Polish workers go, they take cultural traditions with them. As a result, although Polish restaurants and food shops have long been a feature of capital cities in Europe, especially since many Poles fled in World War II, these outlets are now spreading further afield as they find new opportunities for work abroad.

ABOVE Deer have been hunted in the forests of Poland since medieval times.

Church festivals

The Catholic church – a hugely important part of life in Poland throughout its recorded history – retains its influence today. Nearly all Poles regard themselves as Catholics, with 75 per cent of them being regular churchgoers. A symbol of hope, the church helped to preserve traditional feast days and foods and provided something to look forward to in the long dark years of food shortages and repression.

Polish cuisine

In a country where the people have had to battle for independence, it is a matter of national pride that the traditions of Polish cuisine have been so well preserved. Faced with bitterly cold winters, the Poles know how to make expert use of their natural resources to produce hearty and sustaining meals; Polish food is not for slimmers! The Polish toast, "Eat, drink and loosen your belt", is an indication of this serious attitude to the consumption of large quantities of food. Today, the emphasis remains focused on healthy produce and excellent home cooking, where time is taken to make a meal in traditional style. Hospitality is, and has always been, highly valued – "a guest in the house is God in the house", as another Polish saying goes.

Family life – the daily routine

From the shipyard communities of Gdansk in the north to the villages in the Tatra mountains in the south, Polish people take their daily meals seriously. Many dishes require long, slow cooking, and as most meals are eaten at home (restaurants are mainly for special occasions), time must be taken to plan, shop and cook for the family.

Breakfast

Although breakfast can be quite a quick meal – the working day often starts at 8 a.m. – it is still quite substantial.

Poles like to base their morning meal on bread, especially dark rye bread, as a good solid partner to cooked meats, hard-boiled eggs, cheese or jam. In the old days, people ate soup for breakfast, often thickened with grains (kasza) or based on sweetened milk with rice – a sustaining bowl of goodness to start the day. These days the liquid is more likely to be a cup of tea or coffee.

Lunch

Traditionally the main meal of the day in Poland, lunch is often eaten at home, although people who travel long distances to work might take lunch with them. If at all possible, everyone in the family will return home sometime between 1 p.m. and 3 p.m. to eat a two- or three-course meal that is designed to set them up with enough energy for the rest of the day's work.

The first course of this meal is nearly always soup. Poles love hearty vegetable and meat soups, and also make a range of chilled ones for summer. The famous soup borscht (barszcz), based on the beautiful ruby-red colour of beetroot, is a favourite dish, which pleases the eye as well as the stomach. Other favourite appetizers might be fish in aspic or a selection of cold cooked meat and vegetables.

Next comes a sustaining main dish, such as Hunter's Stew (bigos) or pork cutlets served with sauerkraut and other vegetables. This course is generally based on meat, apart from on fasting days ordained by the Catholic ritual, where fish takes its place.

Finally, the Poles love their desserts and will often find room for a cake such as Poppy Seed Cake (makowiec), a substantial pastry such as Plum Dumplings (knedle ze śliwkami), or a dish of ice cream in hot weather.

FAR LEFT There is an abundance of fresh produce available at Polish markets.
LEFT Bakeries selling bread and a range of cakes are visited on a daily basis.

Supper

At the end of the long working day, families will gather together again to eat supper, normally between 6 p.m. and 8 p.m. This is usually a lighter meal than lunch, with similar dishes – soup, fish, sweet desserts – being served, but this time omitting the heavier main course. Both lunch and supper may be accompanied by wine, vodka or fruit juice.

Snacks

Apart from the three main meals of the day, Poles enjoy eating snacks. Many Polish people have a sweet tooth, and to serve the need for something to fill the gap between breakfast and lunch or lunch and supper, there are a multitude of local bakeries in every town and village. These bakeries sell a range of breads, of course, but their speciality is more often the delectable cakes and pastries that are so popular with their clientele.

Many of these delicacies are based on yeast dough, for example doughnuts (pączki z różą) or jam puffs, plum cake and seasonal favourites such as babka, an Easter cake made with citrus fruit, raisins and spices. Other sweet snacks are pastry-based, such as mazurek, a delicious tart made of pastry enriched with egg yolks and topped with all kinds of sweet things – soft cheese, honey, fruits, jam or nuts.

Summer and winter soups

Polish winters are freezing, but the summers can be hot and steamy. To counteract this, there are many Polish dishes designed to cool the body on a hot day, most notably the chilled fruit soups that make the first course of a big meal palatable when it's humid.

These fruit soups are sweetened with sugar or honey, and based on whatever seasonal produce is available – plums, cherries, apples, pears or berries – with the addition of spices such as cinnamon and a spoonful of sour cream (smietanie). There are also cold savoury vegetable soups, based on beetroot and cucumber (chłodnik) or sorrel (zupa szczawiowa), both of which can be served either hot or chilled.

Winter fare is unashamedly hearty. The Poles know that they need good, solid food to withstand the snow and ice that covers the country. Winter soups are based on any meat and vegetables that are available, thickened with potatoes and grains and often served in a hollowed-out loaf of bread. In hard times, this soup may have been the only meal available to hardworking peasants, so it had to be as nutritious as possible.

Today, barley soup (krupnik) is still a national favourite – everyone loves the combination of different vegetables slowly simmered with barley, pieces of pork and herbs in a tasty stock.

ABOVE LEFT Hot doughnuts filled with rosehip jam are a favourite snack in Poland. ABOVE CENTRE Plum dumplings are enjoyed as a dessert throughout the year. ABOVE Steaming, hearty soups are often served in bread as a nourishing winter meal.

Polish vodka

Picasso once said that "the three most astonishing things in the past half-century have been the blues, cubism and Polish vodka". This endorsement is well founded, as the amazingly strong spirit, made from potatoes and selected grains, flavoured with herbs, berries and spices, is now popular around the world and has a reputation for quality. In Poland, vodka is often drunk with meals as well as at other times.

The stove: heart of the home

Polish cooking is often based on long, slow simmering, stewing and baking. For this the predominantly rural population needed a stove with a coal- or wood-fired oven ready for roasting and baking, and a hotplate on top for the stewing pot.

This stove was the focal point of the rural household. It was a normally a huge affair, often large enough for four people to comfortably sleep on top of it in the winter, and leaving a warm hidey-hole between the stove and the wall for children and pets.

From these basic cooking facilities came the most traditional Polish dishes, such as soups, simmered fish and meat stews. Dumplings (*pierogi*) were gently cooked in a large pot over the fire or on the top of the stove, and meat, bread, pastries and cakes were baked in the oven.

RIGHT A shop window in Krakow, displaying a range of pickled and preserved items.

Today, the same techniques and equipment are still used for many favourite recipes, with the addition of a large, heavy frying pan for tossing boiled dumplings cooked in butter before they are served, or for quickly cooking pork chops covered in breadcrumbs (*kotlet schabowy*) or potato pancakes (*placki ziemniaczane*).

Preserving food

In any country that has extremely cold winters and where very little fresh food is available for weeks on end, techniques for preserving food needed to be developed to make sure everyone had enough to eat through the bleak months. This tradition is true in Poland today, and there are a range of pickled foods that feature on the winter menu.

Sauerkraut is perhaps the most famous of these. It originated as a way of preserving cabbage for use when fresh vegetables could not be dug from the snow-covered fields, but has now become a staple ingredient that is used in every weather. In past times, country households would keep a barrel of the pickle in the kitchen, while townspeople could buy a ladleful at a time from a similar barrel in the grocer's shop. Today, it is widely available in jars and cans in supermarkets and grocers.

Other vegetables, such as cucumbers, gherkins, beetroots (beets) and kohlrabi, can also be pickled, while others, such as the many varieties of mushrooms found in the forests, can be dried and added to marinades, soups and stews.

In past years, before fresh fish could be easily and quickly transported around the country, only those people who lived near the coast could eat seafood all year round, until a recipe for soused herring made with pickling spices and vinegar was developed. Like sauerkraut, this is a staple dish that is found in most European countries with a Baltic Sea or North Sea coastline, ranging from Belgium to Norway.

LEFT The oven is the key feature of this elaborately decorated Polish kitchen.

Meat

A feature of most Polish meals, meat, poultry and game are often marinated in a mixture containing spices, such as juniper berries, bay, allspice and cloves, before cooking. This technique was developed to improve flavour and make sure that any tough cuts are tenderized, as well as to mask the unpleasant smell of any meat that is less than fresh.

Pork is the most popular meat, and as in many largely rural countries, a family pig is often carefully reared to provide the country household with food all year round. Extremely versatile, the meat from one pig can be smoked and cured as bacon and ham, or chopped and mixed with spices to make Polish sausages (kiełbasa). These sausages are often eaten as snacks with a glass of vodka, or added to soup or stew for extra flavour and protein.

Dairy foods

As well as being enjoyed fresh, milk is also preserved in various forms in Poland. As milk becomes sour cream, butter and cheese, its flavour develops and changes, and it can be used to add piquancy to savoury and sweet recipes. Sour cream (smietanie) is used so widely that it is sold in large bottles in every food shop.

Regional and ethnic dishes

The shape and terrain of Poland means that it has always been well served by trade links within and through the country. Linked by the mountain ranges to the south to its Czech and Slovak neighbours, and with no geographical barriers further north, Poland trades freely with Germany and France on one side and Russia on the other. With such open borders, any localized recipes soon spread over the whole country.

Despite this, some regions are known for certain foods. The northern lakes produce freshwater fish in abundance, and these became a major part of many Christmas feasts. Further south, fields of grain provide the basic ingredients for all sorts of bread, particularly the dense, robust rye bread found all around Poland and its neighbouring countries. In the high southern mountains, sure-footed sheep provide milk to be made into a fresh, sharp cheese (oszczypek).

The influence of the many Jewish people who lived in Poland before World War II can be seen in several dishes, especially the traditional Jewish fish dish, pike or carp in aspic, which has been incorporated into Polish Catholic tradition and has become a regular part of Christmas feasts.

ABOVE LEFT Pickled herring is a popular appetizer or snack in many Baltic states. ABOVE Sharp, tangy goat's cheese is a speciality of the southern mountains.

White borscht soup (żurek)

This popular light but warming dish is made from a strained vegetable stock with the addition of mushrooms, potatoes and chopped hard-boiled eggs. The "borscht" part of the soup is a fermented rye mixture which needs to be prepared several days in advance. The end result is a pale-coloured soup, which is lent a distinctive taste by the rye borscht, quite different from the better-known dark red beetroot (beet) borscht.

Festivals and celebrations

Many of the festivals celebrated in Poland are linked to the rituals of the Catholic church and the rhythm of the Catholic calendar, with its emphasis on Christmas and Easter. These two major Christian celebrations are marked with a quite magnificent seriousness in Poland, even in these days of commercialism, and the religious basis is never forgotten. Other, more pagan celebrations are also noted during the year, including hunting feasts in rural areas and name day parties everywhere, as well as weddings and christenings. All provide a chance for the family to get together and enjoy themselves, but it's at Christmas and Easter that Polish people pull out all the stops with elaborate feasts and parties.

Christmas

Celebrations start early in Poland, with St Nicholas arriving on his sleigh on 6th December to hand out presents of honey and almond cookies and apples to the children, along with religious pictures of the nativity. Traditionally, good children were rewarded for reciting their prayers to St Nicholas; naughty ones who had not bothered to learn them by heart could expect a severe rebuke, and no presents!

After a few weeks' wait the biggest celebration of the year on Christmas Eve (Wigilia) takes place. Wigilia means "waiting", and it's the anticipation of Christ's birth that is all-important.

This is a huge affair of long meals and family rituals involving dressing the tree and opening gifts. The presence of as many family members as possible is a vital element, and guests and strangers are welcomed in as part of the family, sometimes to make up the numbers – odd numbers at the table are thought to bring bad luck.

In past times, people in rural areas would bring a sheaf of corn into the house or spread hay under the white tablecloth to remind them of the manger in the stable where Jesus was laid. Most of all it's a day for telling the story of the Christmas angel, Aniołek, who brings the presents (and sometimes

the sparkling tree, too) into the house while no one is looking; for dressing up in your best clothes; for waiting for the appearance of the first star in the sky, which signals the beginning of the feast; and, most of all, for eating the traditional food of this special day.

The Wigilia feast

This Christmas Eve meal is a major event in the Polish calendar. No meat is eaten, according to religious tradition, and people even try to avoid using animal fats in the cooking. In past years, the feast was a huge affair of twelve courses (to represent the twelve apostles), but nowadays three or four courses are considered plenty.

First, the family and guests will break and share a plate of opłatek, the thin wafers associated with the communion service in church. There then follows a warming beetroot (beet) or sweet almond soup and some dishes of vegetables from the surrounding fields, such as sauerkraut, stuffed kohlrabi, mushrooms and potatoes. The main dish is usually a magnificent whole carp or pike and the meal ends with a dried fruit compote, and then the special

FAR LEFT Carp in aspic is just one of the many dishes served for the Wigilia feast. LEFT Honey and almond cookies are given to children in the lead-up to Christmas.

pudding, *kutia*, made from wheat grains, honey, poppy seeds, cherry jam, dried fruit and nuts. Those who are still hungry might nibble the traditional honey cookies or a yeasty poppy seed roll, and the grown-ups can open their presents with a glass or two of fiery flavoured vodka to hand.

After the feast
Midnight Mass follows the family celebration, and is a chance to focus on the real reason for the feast and the end of *Wigilia* as the birth of Christ is celebrated in church.

A *Wigilia* feast
This joyful family feast will include some of the following:
- Christmas borscht
- Christmas Eve almond soup
- Herring in sour cream
- Carp in aspic, or wine sauce, or fried in breadcrumbs
- Pike with hard-boiled eggs and parsley
- Dumplings *(pierogi)*
- Sauerkraut with mushrooms
- Noodles with poppy seeds
- Dried fruit compote
- Poppy seed rolls
- Christmas pudding *(kutia)*
- Wine with the savoury dishes and vodka with the pudding

After all this splendour, Christmas Day lunch is often a smaller and quieter affair. Some families eat a roast turkey, but more often the meal consists of leftovers from the previous day served cold with plenty of salad and vegetables. It is a time to enjoy visiting friends or family, where you will certainly be offered a piece of delicious honey cake or cookies.

The end of the Christmas story
On Twelfth Night (6th January), Christmas finally winds down with a quiet celebration. On this day, many families still mark the initials of the three kings above their front door with chalk, and burn incense in order to protect the family against hardship during the coming year.

Easter
It's hard to know how to top the festivities of *Wigilia*, but Polish people certainly try to go one better at Easter *(Wielkanoc)*, when this most important Christian festival is celebrated with lavish feasting and partying alongside the religious ritual.

There is a longer build-up to Easter than at Christmas, starting with the quiet and serious weeks of Lent. During this period everyone tries to give up some favourite food, and meat is eaten far less often than at other times of the year.

ABOVE Polish women and girls traditionally spend Good Friday decorating eggs.

Easter also coincides with the annual spring cleaning season, a ritual that symbolizes death and re-birth. In Holy Week, just before Easter, the cooking and cleaning in every household rises to such a pitch that many men take themselves quietly out of the way to the local tavern or restaurant for a restorative meal or just some shots of excellent vodka.

Easter weekend
On Good Friday, the main focus is on the church. Many families visit several churches, to pray of course, but also to inspect and compare the traditional decorated tombs found in each church, with an effigy of the Christ figure surrounded by flowers. A simple meal will follow that evening – maybe some soused herring and potatoes – and the females spend the day colouring and decorating eggs.

Easter Saturday is a day of anticipation. In past times, the local priest would visit as many houses as possible to bless the family and the Easter feast laid out on the table, ready for the following day's celebrations. Finally, at midday on Easter Sunday, after another church service in the morning, the family gather for a long feast lasting through to the evening.

The Easter Sunday feast

In the centre of the Easter Sunday table there is often a white lamb made of sugar or butter, usually standing on a little hill of greenery made of cress grown specially for the occasion, and surrounded by sweetly scented hyacinths. Once the family has gathered, a plate of quartered hard-boiled eggs is passed around and the feast can begin. This consists of cold meats including sausage, roast pork, turkey and ham; cold vegetables and salads; *mazurki*, the sweet, decorated pastries; and the Easter cake known as *babka*, baked in a special tall tin with fluted edges.

Harvest festival

A traditional rural feast day, harvest festival is celebrated in most parts of the world. In Poland, the most popular and hardworking girl in a village (or maybe just the prettiest?) is chosen to represent the farm workers, and will carry a harvest wreath on her head from church to present to the local landowner. He will then reward the company with an array of dishes containing all the good things gathered in during the harvest – grains, fruit, nuts and plenty of vodka.

ABOVE LEFT Lambs made from sugar or butter are a traditional part of the Easter feast. ABOVE The Easter table is laid on Easter Saturday and is often blessed by a priest.

Secular festivals

Although religious occasions are marked with the best feasts, Poles do celebrate other events throughout the year, following the rhythm of the seasons.

New Year's Eve

This is a time to shake off the excesses of Christmas and start afresh with a party, either at home or out at a restaurant if you are lucky enough to be able to book a place. There may well be a full dinner during the evening, followed by champagne and a cold buffet as the clock strikes twelve.

LEFT The annual harvest is a time of celebration and feasting.

Family occasions

The traditional family celebrations of weddings and christenings are, of course, another good excuse for a great meal with friends and family members, as they are everywhere in the world.

Weddings

In Poland, wedding traditions dictate that the bride and groom must pass a bottle of vodka to their neighbours before they can be allowed to walk through the spectators into the church.

After the ceremony there is a lavish banquet for all the family and friends, and the feasting, dancing, games and singing can begin. Before it starts, however, another little ritual is always carried out, whereby the respective parents of the bride and groom offer them bread (ensuring that they always have plenty to eat); salt (to remind them of the hardships they may have to overcome); and a bottle of champagne (to celebrate the good things in life). The couple then drink the champagne and throw the glasses over their shoulders – if they smash, that will bring good luck.

Christenings

Following a ceremony in church, christening parties often move on to the local tavern, where the godparents are expected to pay for the guests to toast the baby's health with vodka.

These celebrations often used to extend over several days, but in busy modern times they are more likely to take up only one day. The traditional gifts of linen robes and caps for the baby have also changed over the years into gifts of cash – doubtless very welcome for new parents.

Name days

Polish people usually celebrate their name days rather than their birthdays. Most people are called by traditional biblical names, and the corresponding saint's day is usually the most important secular day of the year for each individual.

This day is usually marked by a feast or party, involving a good spread of whatever food is in season, plus plenty of alcohol, chocolates and presents. The guests may also sing the traditional song *"Sto lat"*, wishing them a hundred years of happy life.

Hunting feasts

In the old days, when rich landowners owned large tracts of Polish countryside, they would organize communal hunting parties to spend the day on the trail of wild boar, game birds and other delicacies of the forest. The whole male population of the village would be co-opted to help in shooting or beating, bringing their hunting dogs with them.

After all this effort and fresh air, the hunters would return ready for some good hot food and drink. This appetite, in conjunction with the mixture of meats from the day's hunt, gave rise to the famous Polish hunter's stew *bigos*. This rich and satisfying mixture of different kinds of meat, sauerkraut, mushrooms and stock is well spiced with juniper berries and peppercorns. Today, both hunting and the stew are still popular, accompanied by a glass of chilled vodka.

LEFT A traditional wedding in the mountains to the south of the country.

Classic ingredients

Poland's position on the cusp of the trade routes between eastern and western Europe means that Polish cooks have had access to a fantastic variety of ingredients and have been exposed to other countries' cooking techniques since medieval times. The typical central European climate of variable, humid summers and wet, cold winters gives ideal growing conditions for many seasonal crops and supports the yearly cycle of rearing farm animals for food, resulting in a natural abundance of locally grown produce. What is more, Poland's forests and lakes provide a wonderful bounty of wild foods, such as game, mushrooms and freshwater fish, which are skilfully transformed into a wide range of inspiring, tasty recipes.

Meat, poultry and game

Pork Every part of the pig, including the offal (variety meats), is used in Poland, where it is the meat of choice. Succulent pork chops can be cooked in breadcrumbs *(kotlet schabowy)*, while the lesser cuts are slowly stewed to make a rich and satisfying dish with cabbage and other vegetables, flavoured with herbs and spices. Roast pork is an integral part of hunter's stew *(bigos)*, alongside other roast meats and sausage. Smoked ham and bacon are much enjoyed and are an important source of protein for the winter months, and honey roast ham is eaten especially at the Easter feast.

Pork sausage Polish sausage *(kiełbasa)* is such an important part of the diet that it was one of the first Polish ingredients to make its way abroad with emigrating families. It is added to stews and soups or simply eaten sliced, as a snack, with a glass of vodka. The ingredients of *kielbasa* vary according to what is available, but prime sausage is always made from good quality pork, spices and herbs, mixed together and smoked gently to achieve the right flavour and consistency.

Veal Poles love veal, and especially the cutlets, which they eat in the same way as pork chops, fried in breadcrumbs.

Every part of the animal is used, including the liver and the brains, a luxurious savoury treat when served on toast. The less tender cuts need to be simmered slowly with stock or made into veal stroganoff, with the addition of wild mushrooms for an earthy flavour.

Beef Brought to Poland by the Tartars, who used to tenderize their beef steaks by placing them under the saddle, raw steak tartare is still popular in Poland, although it can only be made from the finest steak. Lesser cuts are better stewed for a long time, as in beef goulash *(gulasz wołowy)*, with the addition of spices and herbs, red wine

BELOW Pork chops make a frequent appearance on the Polish table.

BELOW Smoked sausage can be served in slices with vodka or added to stews.

BELOW Cuts of beef can be chopped and served raw, or slow-cooked with spices.

ABOVE Partridges and other game birds are often marinated before being roasted.

ABOVE The much-loved carp is a key feature of the Christmas Eve feast.

ABOVE Trout are delicious simply baked whole with butter and parsley.

and sour cream. Alternatively, the meat can be flattened, rolled around a mushroom mixture and roasted.

Poultry Chicken is a popular meat in Poland, where many small farmers still keep their own hens for fresh eggs and tasty meat. However, the stronger flavours of goose and turkey are highly prized for special occasions, such as Easter, when the cold roast meat is served. Goose has the additional benefit that, because it releases so much fat in cooking, its meat can be chopped and preserved in airtight jars for the winter with a layer of the melted fat on top to seal in the goodness.

Venison Deer abound in the Polish forests, and a favourite recipe is delicate venison steak simply pan-fried with earthy wild mushrooms and served with a rich sauce made with the juices and a glass of red wine.

Hare A full-flavoured meat, often made into stews, hare is usually marinated for at least 24 hours in a flavoursome mixture of vegetables and buttermilk, spiced with juniper berries. It is then baked, and the strong taste is perfectly balanced by the creaminess in the accompanying sauce.

Wild boar The forests in the north of Poland are still populated by wild boar, which thrive in the extensive woods. The meat is prized for its wonderful flavour, particularly when marinated then simmered in a strong sauce or stock with lots of spices.

Game birds Polish cuisine is full of recipes for partridge, pheasant, quail, pigeon and wild duck. The skill of plucking, dissecting, hanging, marinating and then cooking these wild birds is one that is still found in many Polish kitchens. Juniper berries and other spices and herbs are added to the marinade and the birds are left to absorb all the flavours for at least two days before cooking.

Freshwater fish and seafood
Carp This tasty fish with its barbed mouth is bred in plentiful quantities in the lakes of northern Poland. Carp has become a staple dish of the Christmas feast, and also features regularly on restaurant menus throughout the year, freshly cooked in broth, fried in breadcrumbs, or jellied in aspic as a refreshing treat. A shiny scale from the Christmas Eve carp, hidden in your wallet, is said to guarantee wealth for the coming year.

Pike Like the carp, pike has become a feature of Christmas feasts, where its solid texture compensates for the lack of meat in the meal. Pike is traditionally accompanied by chopped hard-boiled eggs and dressed with fresh parsley, or a rich sauce made with red wine and raisins.

Other freshwater fish Trout, salmon, sturgeon and perch are plentiful in Poland's rivers, particularly in the fast-flowing torrents that descend from the Carpathian mountains in the south. They are often cooked simply with butter in the oven. Eel can be smoked or marinated and then chopped into tasty pieces as an appetizer – its distinctive flavour and soft texture blends well with the local vodka.

Fish from the sea Haddock, sardines and halibut can be found in the Baltic Sea and make fantastic, delicate dishes when served really fresh, fried or grilled (broiled) with just a simple cream sauce and some chopped fresh herbs for accompaniment.

Dairy produce
Sour cream This thick, sharp cream is one of the most popular ingredients of Polish cooking. It is added to all kinds

ABOVE Curd cheese is used to make savoury dumplings and in a range of desserts.

ABOVE Vivid beetroots (beets) are used to make the famous soup *barszcz*.

ABOVE Mushrooms, such as chanterelles, are added to stews or served as a side dish.

of hearty soups and stews, rich desserts, creamy sauces and salad dressings. It blends beautifully into warm dishes, and makes a lovely sauce on its own with chopped hard-boiled eggs and mustard.

Cheese Often made from sheep's milk, which gives it a tangy flavour, cheese is sold in its smoked form, which is eaten as part of a cold buffet, or as curd cheese. Polish cheesecake *(sernik)*, made with curd cheese and eggs and flavoured with lemon, vanilla and sugar, is a great favourite. One of the few savoury recipes containing cheese is stuffed dumplings *(pierogi)*, which uses curd cheese mixed with potato to make a delicious dumpling filling.

Eggs As well as being used in baking, eggs are commonly hard-boiled, chopped and used as a garnish or mixed into a creamy sauce. Cooked eggs make a great thickener for mayonnaise and other cold sauces, and add nutritional value too.

Vegetables and grains
Beetroot (beet) This dark red vegetable is loved by the Poles for its taste and its nutritional qualities, not to mention its reputation as an aphrodisiac!

Beetroot not only makes a lovely hot soup *(barszcz)*, but it also blends beautifully with sour cream and hard-boiled eggs to make a fragrant cold soup *(chłodnik)*.

Potatoes It's surprising that the potato, found in so many Polish recipes, was not grown in Poland until the 17th century. Today it has many uses, including as a thickener in soups, as a main course with mushrooms, and in pancakes and dumplings – all of which are substantial and filling delicacies suitable for the cold weather.

Other root vegetables The Poles also grow and eat carrots, kohlrabi, onions and any other vegetables that can be stored for use during the cold winter months. They all tend to be added to salads, soups and stews rather than being served separately as a side dish.

Salad vegetables When the Italian Queen Bona Sforza brought her retinue to Poland in the early 16th century, she also brought a supply of lighter vegetables and salad ingredients, such as lettuce and leeks, which are still known as *włoszczyzna* ("Italian vegetables"). Polish recipes for appetizers and side dishes are often

based on cold salads and mixtures of fruit and vegetables, such as apple and leek salad, which makes the perfect accompaniment to cold meat and fish.

Sauerkraut The best way to preserve cabbage is by pickling it in brine. This pungent pickle is a staple ingredient, and is used in all sorts of ways in Polish cooking, particularly as a stuffing for dumplings *(pierogi)* and as a tasty addition to soup.

Mushrooms A staple of the Polish kitchen, mushrooms grow wild in the forests of Poland, and most rural people know which ones to pick for cooking. Their strong, earthy flavour goes well with robust Polish dishes, for instance in a rich wild boar casserole or a sturdy, filling soup with pasta. Dried mushrooms are also a popular addition to soups or stews.

Grains Buckwheat, wheat, millet, barley and rye are grown on the flat arable fields of central Poland. The porridge-like dish, *kasza*, is made from grains simmered in water, with the addition of honey for a sweet dish, or bacon fat and salt to make it a savoury and filling accompaniment for the meat course. Polish bread tends to be either very white – used for breadcrumbs as well as for breakfast – or very dark, made from rye and with a strong taste.

Seasonings

Poppy seeds These aromatic little black seeds are added to many dishes for decoration and flavour. Poppy seed cake (makowiec) is a favourite at any time, but particularly at Christmas.

Juniper berries Traditionally the main flavouring in marinades for game, these small dried berries have a pungent, spicy flavour that lends a distinctive note to meat and sauces.

Paprika This mild, peppery spice is made from ground capsicums and was originally brought to Poland from South America on the spice trading routes through Europe. It adds an orangey-red colour and a gentle piquancy to dishes.

Other spices Cinnamon and cloves are often used in both savoury and sweet dishes, particularly for flavouring marinades or a compote of dried fruit. Vanilla is added to many desserts and cakes, including the Easter speciality cake, babka wielkanocna. Allspice, with its peppery flavour, livens up a marinade for meat.

BELOW Cinnamon, cloves and bay leaves are key flavourings in marinades.

Horseradish This root has a strong, bitter taste. It is freshly grated and mixed with stock or sour cream for a robust sauce that goes well with game.

Dill The most important herb in Polish cooking, dill grows well in the damp climate, and its feathery fronds and aniseed flavour complement fish and vegetable dishes.

Parsley and other herbs Many green herbs flourish in the Polish climate, including marjoram, chives, bay leaves and parsley. They are used to add flavour and colour to soups and stews, or for rubbing into the skin of a roast chicken or other roasted meat. Parsley makes a pretty garnish when sprinkled on top of a dish.

Sweet things

Fruit Fresh and dried fruits abound in the Polish diet. Delectable seasonal fruits – raspberries, strawberries, peaches, plums, apples, pears, grapes – can be eaten as they are, made into delicious desserts with the addition of honey or sugar, or included in cakes and pastries. They are also mixed with spices and sour cream to make fruit soup, dried and added to marinades for game, and soaked to make a fruit drink.

BELOW Plums and other orchard fruits often feature in desserts and cakes.

Honey Sweet, aromatic honey has a special affinity with the Christmas feast in the form of honey and almond cookies and angel's wings (chrusty). Honey is also added to vodka or fruit juice with cinnamon and cloves for a delicious Christmas drink.

Alcoholic drinks

Vodka Polish vodka is famous for its remarkable taste and strength. It is a favourite drink all over Poland, as an accompaniment to a meal or on its own with a slice or two of kiełbasa, Polish sausage. Poles are justifiably proud of their delicious flavoured vodkas, which are now exported all over the world.

Beer Polish beer began to be brewed on a large scale in the 19th century, when it was mainly the dark, strong, sweet kind known as porter. More recently the Poles have started to brew lighter (but still strongly alcoholic) lager beers that are based on the Czech model.

Mead Mead was the alcoholic drink of choice in past times, when honey was more accessible than hops. These days honey is more often used to make fruit punch, a non-alcoholic drink that warms the body in the chilly winter.

BELOW Versatile and delicious, honey can be used in baking or to make drinks.

SOUPS AND APPETIZERS

Wild Mushroom Soup with
Home-made Pasta

Christmas Eve Almond Soup

Sorrel Soup with Eggs

Red Borscht Soup

White Borscht Soup

Chicken Soup with Noodles

Potato Pancakes

Polish-style Herrings

Hare and Calf's Liver Terrine

Light and warming

Soup is an important part of Polish cuisine. It can be a thin, tasty appetizer before a meal, or a sustaining meal in a bowl, such as Chicken Soup with Noodles *(Rosół z makaronem)*. The subtle, often spicy flavours of vegetable soups are a real speciality of the Polish kitchen, the most famous of which is Red Borscht *(Czerwony barszcz)*, a glowing soup made from fragrant beetroots (beets). Pale, tasty White Borscht *(Żurek)* – an intriguing soup made from vegetable stock and a fermented rye mixture, garnished with chopped hard-boiled eggs – is less well known outside Poland.

Other favourite appetizers include Polish-style Herrings *(Śledź w śmietanie)*, a popular dish in which fish are marinated in spices and sour cream, and, of course, Potato Pancakes *(Placki ziemniaczane)*, a tasty snack made with grated and fried potatoes.

Wild Mushroom Soup with Home-made Pasta
Zupa ze świeżych grzybów

Rich and earthy, wild mushroom soups have been made in Poland since the Middle Ages. This fragrant version is served with sour cream, chopped fresh herbs and delicate flakes of home-made pasta, making it both sustaining and delicious.

Serves 4
50g/2oz/1 cup dried mushrooms, preferably ceps
1.5 litres/2½ pints/6¼ cups water
1 carrot, roughly chopped
1 parsnip, roughly chopped
½ celeriac, roughly chopped
1 large onion, roughly chopped
15g/½oz/1 tbsp butter
6–8 black peppercorns
juice of 1 lemon
salt, to taste
sour cream and chopped fresh parsley or dill, to garnish

For the pasta
115g/4oz/1 cup plain (all-purpose) flour, plus extra for sprinkling
1 egg, beaten
2.5ml/½ tsp salt
15–30ml/1–2 tbsp water

1 Rinse the dried mushrooms, then place in a large pan with the water, heat until warm and leave to soak for 30 minutes.

2 Bring the pan to the boil. Cover and simmer for 25–30 minutes, or until the mushrooms are soft. Strain the stock into a clean pan, reserving the mushrooms.

3 Meanwhile, make the pasta. Sift the flour into a large bowl, then make a well in the centre and add the egg, salt and 15ml/1 tbsp water.

4 Mix to combine, adding more water if necessary, then transfer the dough to a lightly floured surface and knead for about 5 minutes, or until the dough is firm.

5 Roll out the dough as thinly as possible, then sprinkle the surface with flour and leave to dry out.

6 Add the carrot, parsnip, celeriac, onion, butter, peppercorns and salt to taste to the pan containing the mushroom stock. Simmer gently over a low heat for a further 20 minutes.

7 Strain the stock into a clean pan, reserving the mushrooms, but discarding the other vegetables. Slice the mushrooms into thin strips.

8 Cut the pasta dough into 1cm/½in squares. Bring a large pan of lightly salted water to the boil, add the pasta squares and cook for about 4 minutes. Drain, rinse in cold water, then drain again.

9 Bring the stock back to the boil, then add the lemon juice, mushrooms and cooked pasta, and heat through.

10 Ladle the soup into warm bowls, then swirl a little sour cream in the centre of each and garnish with chopped parsley or dill.

PER SERVING: Energy 265kcal/1111kJ; Protein 7.4g; Carbohydrate 31.3g, of which sugars 0.9g; Fat 13.2g, of which saturates 7.4g; Cholesterol 75mg; Calcium 72mg; Fibre 2.4g; Sodium 343mg.

Serves 4
500ml/17fl oz/generous 2 cups milk
225g/8oz/2 cups ground almonds
115g/4oz/1 cup cooked rice
  (50g/2oz/¼ cup raw weight)
a drop of almond extract
50g/2oz/¼cup currants
  or raisins
15ml/1 tbsp sugar (optional)
4 egg yolks (optional)

Christmas Eve Almond Soup
Zupa migdałowa

A traditional part of the Christmas Eve feast, this nourishing, slightly sweet almond soup is made with rice and currants and is often served with an egg yolk. It makes a hearty appetizer for a winter meal, or can be eaten on its own as a snack.

1 Bring the milk to the boil in a large, heavy pan. Add the ground almonds, stir and cook gently, stirring often, over a low heat for 15–20 minutes, or until slightly thick.

2 Mix together the rice, almond extract, currants or raisins and sugar, if using.

3 Place a heaped tablespoon of the rice mixture in the base of each of four bowls.

4 Ladle the soup into the bowls. If you like, place a raw egg yolk on top of each serving and serve immediately.

COOK'S TIP
You may find that the dried fruit gives the soup enough sweetness for your taste, in which case omit the added sugar.

PER SERVING: Energy 480kcal/1999kJ; Protein 17.3g; Carbohydrate 28.2g, of which sugars 16.7g; Fat 33.6g, of which saturates 3.8g; Cholesterol 7mg; Calcium 299mg; Fibre 4.4g; Sodium 64mg.

Serves 4

15ml/1 tbsp butter
400g/14oz fresh sorrel leaves, chopped
15ml/1 tbsp plain (all-purpose) flour
1 litre/1¾ pints/4 cups beef or
  vegetable stock
45–60ml/3–4 tbsp sour cream
4 hard-boiled eggs, chopped
salt and ground black pepper,
  to taste

Sorrel Soup with Eggs
Zupa szczawiowa z jajkiem

Sorrel grows wild in grassy areas in Poland, but it is also cultivated commercially for use in a range of dishes, including soups, sauces and salads. It has a pleasant, slightly sour taste, which is complemented by the richness of the sour cream and hard-boiled eggs in this dish.

1 Melt the butter in a large pan, then add the chopped sorrel leaves and a pinch of salt.

2 Cook the sorrel gently over a low heat for 5–7 minutes, until the leaves have just wilted.

3 Put the flour in a small bowl and gradually add 60ml/4 tbsp stock, mixing constantly to make a paste. Add to the pan and stir to combine.

4 Stir in the remaining stock, bring to the boil and simmer for 10 minutes.

5 Season to taste with salt and ground black pepper, then gradually add the sour cream, whisking well between each addition.

6 Transfer the soup to warmed soup bowls and top with a spoonful of chopped hard-boiled egg.

VARIATION
If you are unable to find sorrel leaves, you could use rocket (arugula) or large basil leaves, although this will alter the flavour.

PER SERVING: Energy 162kcal/673kJ; Protein 9.8g; Carbohydrate 5g, of which sugars 2g; Fat 11.7g, of which saturates 5g; Cholesterol 205mg; Calcium 215mg; Fibre 2.2g; Sodium 238mg.

Red Borscht Soup
Czerwony Barszcz

Borscht made with red beetroot has been an intrinsic part of Polish cuisine for centuries, with the oldest known recipe dating back to the 16th century. There are two versions: borscht for the Christmas Eve feast, and this one for Easter made with fermented juice.

Serves 4–6

1kg/2¼ lb beef bones
1 leek, roughly chopped
1 large onion, roughly chopped
2 slices of celeriac or parsnip
2 carrots, roughly chopped
5ml/1 tsp salt
5–6 dried wild mushrooms, rinsed and
   soaked in warm water for 30 minutes
juice of ½ lemon (optional)
pinch of sugar (optional)
175ml/16fl oz/¾ cup dry red wine (optional)
1 garlic clove, crushed (optional)
chopped fresh dill, to garnish
Dumplings Stuffed with Mushrooms
   (see page 92), to serve

For the fermented beetroot juice

1.8kg/4lb raw red beetroots (beets)
1.5 litres/2½ pints/6¼ cups boiled water,
   allowed to cool until just lukewarm
1 slice wholegrain (whole-wheat) bread
4–5 garlic cloves, peeled
10 black peppercorns
4–5 allspice berries
2–3 bay leaves

COOK'S TIP
Red Borscht is sometimes served in a cup as a drink during a wedding, or as a hangover cure after a party.

1 To make the fermented beetroot juice, carefully wash the beetroots, then peel and slice thinly. Place them in a large glass jar or a bowl and cover completely with the lukewarm water.

2 Place the bread on top, then add the garlic, peppercorns, allspice and bay leaves. Cover the jar or bowl with a piece of muslin (cheesecloth) and put in a warm place. Leave to ferment for 3 days.

3 Skim off the foam that will have risen to the surface and strain the ruby-red juice into a bowl, then transfer to clean bottles or jars. Cork and keep in a cool place until required. (It will keep for several months, if stored in a cool place.)

4 Put the bones in a large pan, pour over 600ml/1 pint/2½ cups of water and add the chopped vegetables and salt. Bring to the boil and simmer for 15 minutes, or until the vegetables are cooked.

5 Meanwhile, put the dried mushrooms and 475ml/16fl oz/2 cups water in a separate pan, bring to the boil and simmer for 5 minutes, or until the mushrooms are cooked.

6 Strain the meat stock and the mushroom cooking liquid into a measuring jug (cup) to measure the final quantity. Pour into a large, clean pan, and add 600ml/1 pint/2½ cups of fermented beetroot juice for every 300ml/½ pint/1¼ cups stock. Heat gently until the borscht just boils, then remove from the heat.

7 Taste the borscht and add lemon juice or sugar, according to your preference. To enhance the acidity, add a glass of red wine, or for extra flavour and aroma, add crushed garlic about 15 minutes before serving.

8 Serve in warmed bowls with Dumplings Stuffed with Mushrooms, garnished with chopped fresh dill.

PER SERVING: Energy 84kcal/348kJ; Protein 0.5g; Carbohydrate 0.5g, of which sugars 0.1g; Fat 9g, of which saturates 3.4g; Cholesterol 8mg; Calcium 2mg; Fibre 0g; Sodium 672mg.

Serves 4

1 celeriac, roughly chopped
3 carrots, roughly chopped
1 leek, roughly chopped
1 onion
2 parsley sprigs
4 garlic cloves, crushed
4 bay leaves
1.2 litres/2 pints/5 cups water
5–6 dried wild mushrooms, rinsed and
   soaked in warm water for 30 minutes
4 small boiled potatoes, cubed
2 hard-boiled eggs, cut into quarters
salt and ground black pepper, to taste
chopped fresh marjoram or dill, to garnish

For the white borscht
50g/2oz/2 cups rye flour
1 rye-bread crust

White Borscht Soup
Żurek

This light, sour soup is made from a fermented rye flour mixture, which needs to be prepared several days before you want to make the soup.

1 To make the white borscht, put the rye flour in a large, heatproof bowl and stir in enough boiling water until the flour forms a thin paste. Leave it to cool, then add 1.2 litres/2 pints/ 5 cups lukewarm water and the bread crust.

2 Transfer to a large, sterile glass jar, cover with muslin (cheesecloth), then close the lid and leave to ferment in a warm place for at least 3 days.

3 To make the stock, put the celeriac, carrots, leek, onion, parsley, garlic, bay leaves and water in a large pan.

4 Bring to the boil, then simmer for 15–20 minutes, or until the vegetables are tender. Strain, discarding the vegetables.

5 Add the dried, soaked mushrooms and 600ml/1 pint/2½ cups of the white borscht to the hot stock. Bring to the boil, then season to taste.

6 Add the chopped potatoes and quartered hard-boiled eggs. Serve immediately, garnished with fresh marjoram or dill.

PER SERVING: Energy 133kcal/561kJ; Protein 6g; Carbohydrate 19.1g, of which sugars 1.5g; Fat 4.2g, of which saturates 0.9g; Cholesterol 95mg; Calcium 26mg; Fibre 1.1g; Sodium 1109mg.

Chicken Soup with Noodles
Rosół z makaronem

This clear chicken broth was traditionally served every Sunday in Poland. Comforting and nutritious, it makes an ideal appetizer, or can be served as a light meal.

Serves 4

1 small chicken, weighing about
  1.6–1.8kg /3½–4lb
2 litres/3½ pints/8¾ cups water
a pinch of salt
10 black peppercorns
1 large onion, chopped
3 carrots, chopped
2 garlic cloves, chopped
2 parsnips, chopped
4 celery sticks, chopped
165g/5½oz egg noodles, to serve
chopped fresh parsley, to garnish

COOK'S TIPS
• If the soup is too fatty for your liking, allow the soup to cool, then chill in the refrigerator. Remove the solidified fat from the top, then gently reheat the soup.
• If it is cloudy, add a piece of raw beetroot (beet) at the end of the cooking time.

1 Cut the chicken into pieces. Put the pieces in a large pan and pour in the water.

2 Bring to the boil, then cover the pan and simmer over a low heat for about 1½ hours.

3 With a slotted spoon skim off any scum or fat that rises to the surface during the cooking time.

4 Remove the chicken from the pan and cut or pull off the meat.

5 Return the meat to the pan and discard the bones.

6 Add the salt, peppercorns, onion, carrots, garlic, parsnips and celery to the pan, and cook over a medium heat for a further 30 minutes, or until the vegetables are tender.

7 Cook the noodles according to the packet instructions, then divide among warm soup bowls.

8 Ladle the soup over the noodles and serve immediately, garnished with chopped parsley.

PER SERVING: Energy 427kcal/1805kJ; Protein 54.5g; Carbohydrate 40.2g, of which sugars 7.8g; Fat 6.4g, of which saturates 1.7g; Cholesterol 152mg; Calcium 76mg; Fibre 5.3g; Sodium 237mg.

Serves 4–6

4–5 large potatoes, peeled and grated
1 large onion, grated
2 eggs
60ml/4 tbsp plain (all-purpose) flour
salt and ground black pepper (optional)
120ml/4fl oz/½ cup melted bacon fat or oil
sour cream and paprika, or sugar, or
  apple sauce to serve

Potato Pancakes
Placki ziemniaczane

This dish was especially popular during World War II, when there was little to buy in the shops, and it was served as a treat for children. Today, these pancakes are still eaten, and taste delicious with sugar, apple sauce, or sour cream and a dash of paprika.

1 Rinse the grated potatoes and onion, then squeeze in your hands to remove the excess liquid.

2 Put the potatoes and onion in a large bowl with the eggs, flour, and salt and pepper if serving with a savoury topping. Mix with your hands to combine thoroughly.

3 Put the bacon fat or oil in a large, heavy frying pan and heat over a high heat until it is almost smoking.

4 Carefully put a large spoonful of the potato mixture into the pan and flatten it slightly with a fork. Repeat until you have about four pancakes in the pan.

5 Fry each pancake until it is golden brown on both sides, then remove from the pan with a slotted spoon and drain on kitchen paper.

6 Keep the cooked pancakes warm in a low oven while you cook the rest of the mixture in the same way.

7 Serve the pancakes warm, with a topping of your choice.

PER SERVING: Energy 291kcal/1221kJ; Protein 6g; Carbohydrate 35.4g, of which sugars 2.9g; Fat 15g, of which saturates 2.2g; Cholesterol 63mg; Calcium 36mg; Fibre 2.1g; Sodium 42mg.

Serves 4

4 medium herrings, cleaned,
  or 8 boneless fillets
2 large onions, thinly sliced
2 lemons, cut into thin slices
10 black peppercorns
5 allspice berries
4 bay leaves, broken into pieces
juice of 3 lemons
150ml/¼ pint/⅔ cup sour cream
2.5ml/½ tsp sugar
4 large potatoes, peeled and sliced
¼ tsp caraway seeds
90ml/6 tbsp vegetable oil
salt and ground black pepper,
  to taste
chopped fresh parsley, to garnish
lemon wedges, to serve

Polish-style Herrings
Śledź w śmietanie

Herrings, prepared in many different ways, are a firm favourite in Poland. They are particularly popular during Lent, on Christmas Eve and on Ash Wednesday, when meat is not allowed. This dish of herrings marinated with spices can be made in advance and kept for a week.

1 Soak the herrings in cold water for at least 24 hours and up to 36 hours, changing the water several times.

2 Drain the water and carefully remove the skin by sliding a sharp knife just under the skin's surface.

3 If using whole herrings, cut off the head and tail. Divide the fish into fillets and remove all the bones, using tweezers or your fingers.

4 Place a layer of fillets in the base of a large glass jar with a lid, then add a thin layer of onions and lemon slices, some peppercorns, allspice berries and bay leaf.

5 Add another layer of herring fillets, and repeat the process until you have used all the ingredients.

6 In a small bowl, mix together the lemon juice, sour cream and sugar, then pour the mixture into the jar.

7 Screw on the lid and shake well so that the sour cream mixture covers the fillets evenly. Leave to marinate in a cool place for 24–36 hours.

8 Preheat the oven to 200°C/400°F/Gas 6. Layer the potatoes in a greased ovenproof dish, sprinkle over the caraway seeds, drizzle with vegetable oil and season to taste. Bake for 35–40 minutes, until the potatoes are tender and golden.

9 Spoon the marinated herrings on to four serving plates and garnish with chopped parsley. Serve with the hot potatoes and lemon wedges for squeezing.

PER SERVING: Energy 508kcal/2098kJ; Protein 19.5g; Carbohydrate 5.4g, of which sugars 4.2g; Fat 45.5g, of which saturates 10.9g; Cholesterol 73mg; Calcium 108mg; Fibre 0.7g; Sodium 137mg.

Hare and Calf's Liver Terrine
Pasztet z wątroby zajęcznej i cielęcej

Hare and other furred game is popular all over Poland, where it has been hunted and cooked for centuries. For tender meat and a good flavour, use young hare that has been hung for at least a week. However, you can use slightly older animals for this terrine, since the meat is minced finely and then combined with other ingredients.

Serves 4–6

5 dried mushrooms, rinsed and soaked
  in warm water for 30 minutes
saddle, thighs, liver, heart and lungs
  of 1 hare
2 onions, cut into wedges
1 carrot, chopped
1 parsnip, chopped
4 bay leaves
10 allspice berries
300g/11oz calf's liver
165g/5½oz unsmoked streaky (fatty)
  bacon rashers (strips)
75g/3oz/1½ cups soft white
  breadcrumbs
4 eggs
105ml/7 tbsp 95 per cent proof Polish
  spirit or vodka
5ml/1 tsp freshly grated nutmeg
10ml/2 tsp dried marjoram
10g/¼oz juniper berries
4 garlic cloves, crushed
150g/5oz smoked streaky (fatty)
  bacon rashers (strips)
salt and ground black pepper,
  to taste
redcurrant jelly and salad,
  to serve

1 Drain the mushrooms and slice into strips. Put the pieces of hare in a large pan and pour in enough water to just cover. Add the onions, carrot, parsnip, mushrooms, bay leaves and allspice. Bring to the boil, then cover and simmer gently for 1 hour. Add a pinch of salt and allow the meat to cool in the stock.

2 Slice the liver and 50g/2oz unsmoked bacon into small pieces and put in a medium pan. Add a ladleful of the stock and simmer for 15 minutes.

3 Preheat the oven to 180°C/350°F/Gas 4. Put two ladlefuls of the stock in a small bowl, add the breadcrumbs and leave to soak.

4 Remove the hare pieces, liver and bacon from the stock and chop finely with a large knife. Transfer to a large bowl, then add the soaked breadcrumbs, eggs, Polish spirit or vodka, nutmeg, marjoram, juniper berries and crushed garlic. Season to taste and mix well to combine thoroughly.

5 Line a 1.2 litre/2 pint/5 cup ovenproof dish with the smoked and remaining unsmoked bacon rashers, making sure they overhang the edges. Spoon in the meat mixture and bring the overhanging bacon over the top. Cover with buttered baking parchment, then cover with a lid or foil.

6 Place the dish in a roasting pan containing boiling water, then put in the oven and bake for 1½ hours, or until a skewer pushed into the centre comes out clean and the juices run clear. Remove the baking parchment and lid or foil about 15 minutes before the end of cooking to allow the terrine to brown.

7 Remove from the oven, and take the dish out of the roasting pan. Cover the terrine with baking parchment and a board and weight down with a 900g/2lb weight (such as two cans). Leave to cool, then turn out on to a serving dish. Serve in slices with redcurrant jelly and a green salad.

PER SERVING: Energy 370kcal/1544kJ; Protein 25g; Carbohydrate 14.1g, of which sugars 2.5g; Fat 18.1g, of which saturates 6.4g; Cholesterol 291mg; Calcium 52mg; Fibre 1.3g; Sodium 851mg.

FISH

Foil-baked Salmon

Baked Trout with Garlic Butter

Grilled Sardines with Parsley

Halibut Steaks with
Lemon Butter

Haddock with Dill Sauce

Haddock and Beer Casserole

Pike with Hard-boiled Eggs

Fried Carp in Breadcrumbs

Carp with Horseradish Sauce

Carp in Wine Sauce

Moist and delicate

Freshwater fish are well represented in Polish cuisine since the country has an abundance of lakes and rivers, but only a short sea coast. The fish of the lakes, especially pike and carp, which live at the bottom of deep, still pools, must be cleaned to get rid of the muddy taste.

Although fish will never supersede meat as the favourite choice for a main course, many dishes, such as Pike with Hard-boiled Eggs *(Szczupak po polsku)* come into their own at Christmas and Easter, and during Lent, when Catholics abstain from eating meat. During the rest of the year fish is fried, grilled (broiled) or baked and served with butter and herbs, as in Halibut Steaks with Lemon Butter *(Steak halibuta z masłem cytrynowym)*. It is also delicious simmered with a robust sauce to bring out the flavour, as in Haddock and Beer Casserole *(Łupacz po polsku)*.

Serves 6

1 salmon, about 1kg/2¼lb,
 cleaned and trimmed
1 small bunch fresh dill, roughly chopped
4 garlic cloves, finely chopped
115g/4oz/½ cup unsalted (sweet) butter
50ml/2fl oz/¼ cup dry white wine
juice of ½ lemon
10–12 black peppercorns
4–5 fresh bay leaves
salt and ground black pepper, to taste
slices of lemon, to garnish
boiled new potatoes and Polish-style
 Cucumber Salad (see page 95), to serve

COOK'S TIPS

• When buying salmon, look for fish with bright, silvery scales and bright red gills.
• Be careful not to overcook salmon, or the flesh will become dry.

Foil-baked Salmon
Cały łosoś pieczony

Baking the whole salmon in a foil package ensures that the flesh remains wonderfully moist. It can be served hot, with new potatoes and cucumber salad, or cold with a salad, for a summer lunch.

1 Preheat the oven to 200°C/400°F/ Gas 6. Place the salmon in the centre of a large piece of foil.

2 In a small bowl, mix together the dill, garlic and butter, to form a smooth paste. Add the wine and lemon juice, and mix to combine.

3 Spread the mixture inside the cavity of the fish, and all over the outside. Put the peppercorns and bay leaves inside the cavity, then season the skin with salt and pepper, to taste.

4 Bring the edges of the foil up and seal to make a loose parcel.

5 Put the fish in the preheated oven and cook for about 30–40 minutes, or until the fish is tender and cooked.

6 Remove from the oven and divide the fish into 6 portions. Transfer to warmed plates.

7 Pour over any juices caught in the foil, and serve immediately with boiled new potatoes and Polish-style Cucumber Salad.

PER SERVING: Energy 242kcal/1005kJ; Protein 20.3g; Carbohydrate 0.1g, of which sugars 0.1g; Fat 17.9g, of which saturates 6.2g; Cholesterol 68mg; Calcium 23mg; Fibre 0g; Sodium 96mg.

Serves 4

2 garlic cloves, crushed

50g/2oz/¼ cup butter, softened,
  plus extra, for greasing

4 medium-sized trout, about 300g/11oz
  each, cleaned and gutted

45ml/3 tbsp lemon juice

salt and ground black pepper, to taste

lemon wedges and fresh parsley sprigs,
  to garnish

Baked Trout with Garlic Butter
Swieży pstrąg w masłem czosnkowym

The rivers in Poland abound with trout, making them a popular choice in a country with only one seaboard. In this delicious recipe they are simply baked in the oven, drizzled with hot garlic butter and served with sprigs of parsley and wedges of lemon.

1 Mix together the garlic and butter in a bowl. Set aside until required.

2 Preheat the oven to 200°C/400°F/ Gas 6. Grease a large baking dish.

3 Place the fish in the baking dish. Pour the lemon juice all over and inside the trout, then season with salt and pepper and put in the oven.

4 Bake the trout for 15–20 minutes, or until the flesh flakes easily when you insert the point of a sharp knife. Place on warm serving plates.

5 Melt the garlic butter in a pan, then pour over the fish. Garnish with lemon and parsley, and serve immediately.

PER SERVING: Energy 205kcal/853kJ; Protein 19.5g; Carbohydrate 0.1g, of which sugars 0.1g; Fat 14.1g, of which saturates 6.5g; Cholesterol 27mg; Calcium 11mg; Fibre 0g; Sodium 132mg.

Serves 4

900g/2lb fresh sardines,
  gutted and scaled

30ml/2 tbsp melted butter or
  vegetable oil

salt and ground black pepper,
  to taste

60ml/4 tbsp chopped fresh parsley,
  to garnish

lemon wedges, to serve

Grilled Sardines with Parsley
Sardynki z rusztu z pietruszką

Sardines are easy to cook, good value for money and extremely tasty, so it is little wonder that they are popular in Poland. Here, they are simply grilled and served with lemon wedges to squeeze over. This recipe also works well on a barbecue.

1 Preheat the grill (broiler) to high. Wash the prepared sardines under cold running water and pat dry on kitchen paper.

2 Brush the fish with melted butter or oil, then season to taste with salt and pepper.

3 Place the sardines on the grill pan and put under the preheated grill. Cook for about 3–4 minutes on each side, until the skin begins to brown.

4 Transfer the sardines to warmed plates, sprinkle with parsley, and serve immediately with lemon wedges.

PER SERVING: Energy 327kcal/1362kJ; Protein 35g; Carbohydrate 0.3g, of which sugars 0.3g; Fat 20.5g, of which saturates 8g; Cholesterol 16mg; Calcium 192mg; Fibre 0.5g; Sodium 240mg.

Serves 4

4 halibut steaks, about
185g/6½oz each
150g/5oz/10 tbsp butter, softened
30ml/2 tbsp chopped fresh parsley
30ml/2 tbsp lemon juice
salt and ground black pepper,
to taste
lemon wedges, to serve
parsley sprigs, to garnish (optional)

Halibut Steaks with Lemon Butter
Steak halibuta z masłem cytrynowym

Poles often simply grill or fry fresh fish, and this elegant dish is a good example. Spreading the steaks with parsley, lemon and butter before cooking ensures the flesh is moist and enables the flavours to permeate the fish without overpowering its delicate flavour.

1 Preheat the grill (broiler) to medium. Season the fish with salt and pepper on both sides.

2 Mix together the butter, parsley and lemon juice, then spread over both sides of each fish steak.

3 Line a grill pan with foil, then put the steaks on the foil. Place under the grill and cook for 7–8 minutes on each side, until tender.

4 Transfer to warmed plates. Serve immediately, with lemon wedges for squeezing over, and garnished with parsley sprigs if using.

PER SERVING: Energy 464kcal/1928kJ; Protein 38.2g; Carbohydrate 0.6g, of which sugars 0.5g; Fat 34.3g, of which saturates 20.1g; Cholesterol 141mg; Calcium 83mg; Fibre 0.6g; Sodium 337mg.

Serves 4

50g/2oz/¼ cup butter
4 haddock fillets, about 185g/6½oz each
200ml/7fl oz/scant 1 cup milk
200ml/7fl oz/scant 1 cup fish stock
3–4 bay leaves
75ml/5 tbsp plain (all-purpose) flour
150ml/¼ pint/⅔ cup double (heavy) cream
1 egg yolk
30ml–45ml/2–3 tbsp chopped fresh dill
salt and ground black pepper, to taste
dill fronds and slices of lemon,
  to garnish (optional)

COOK'S TIP
A member of the cod family, silver-skinned haddock is sold whole, as steaks or as fillets. It is suitable for grilling (broiling), frying or smoking.

Haddock with Dill Sauce
Łupacz gotowany

Dill is Poland's favourite herb, and here it is used to lift the simple cream sauce that accompanies the moist fillets of poached haddock. Serve on its own, or with seasonal vegetables.

1 Melt 25g/1oz/2 tbsp butter in a frying pan, then add the haddock fillets, milk, fish stock, bay leaves, and salt and pepper to taste.

2 Bring to a simmer, then poach the fish gently over a low heat for 10–15 minutes until tender.

3 Meanwhile, melt the remaining butter in a small pan, add the flour and cook, stirring, for 2 minutes.

4 Remove the pan from the heat and slowly add the double cream, whisking constantly.

5 Stir in the egg yolk and chopped dill, then return to the heat and simmer for 4 minutes, or until the sauce has thickened. Do not allow the sauce to boil. Season to taste with salt and pepper.

6 Remove the haddock fillets to a serving dish or warmed plates and pour over the hot sauce.

7 Garnish the fish with dill fronds and slices of lemon, if you like, and serve immediately.

PER SERVING: Energy 503kcal/2097kJ; Protein 36.6g; Carbohydrate 15.5g, of which sugars 1.2g; Fat 33.2g, of which saturates 19.6g; Cholesterol 191mg; Calcium 92mg; Fibre 1g; Sodium 207mg.

Serves 4

150g/5oz/2 cups wild mushrooms

50g/2oz/¼ cup butter

2 large onions, roughly chopped

2 celery sticks, sliced

2 carrots, sliced

4 haddock steaks, about
 185g/6½oz each

300ml/½ pint/1¼ cups light lager

4 bay leaves

25g/1oz/¼ cup plain (all-purpose) flour

200ml/7fl oz/scant 1 cup double
 (heavy) cream

salt and ground black pepper,
 to taste

dill sprigs, to garnish

Haddock and Beer Casserole
Łupacz po polsku

The earthy flavour of wild mushrooms perfectly complements the delicate taste of the haddock steaks and creamy sauce in this satisfying dish. Cooking it in beer ensures that the flesh is moist and makes a distinctive and delicious addition to the sauce.

1 Preheat the oven to 190°C/375°F/ Gas 5. Brush the wild mushrooms to remove any grit and only wash the caps briefly if necessary. Dry with kitchen paper and chop them.

2 Melt 25g/1oz/2 tbsp butter in a flameproof casserole, then add the onions, mushrooms, celery and carrots. Fry for about 8 minutes, or until golden brown.

3 Place the haddock steaks on top of the vegetables, then pour over the lager. Add the bay leaves and season well with salt and pepper.

4 Put the casserole in the preheated oven and cook for 20–25 minutes, or until the fish flakes easily when tested.

5 Remove the fish and vegetables from the casserole with a slotted spoon and transfer to a serving dish. Cover and keep warm while you make the sauce.

6 Melt the remaining butter in a medium pan, then stir in the flour and cook, stirring, for 2 minutes.

7 Pour in the liquid from the casserole, mix well and simmer for 2–3 minutes.

8 Add the double cream to the sauce and heat briefly, without boiling.

9 Serve the fish and vegetables on warmed plates, with the sauce poured over and garnished with sprigs of dill.

PER SERVING: Energy 564kcal/2346kJ; Protein 37g; Carbohydrate 17.9g, of which sugars 10.5g; Fat 38.8g, of which saturates 23.5g; Cholesterol 158mg; Calcium 106mg; Fibre 3.4g; Sodium 231mg.

Serves 4

2 carrots, roughly chopped
2 parsnips, roughly chopped
¼ celery stick, roughly chopped
1 leek, roughly chopped
1 large onion, roughly chopped
4–5 black peppercorns
2–3 bay leaves
1.8kg/4lb pike, cleaned, scaled and
   cut into 4 steaks
25g/1oz/2 tbsp butter
3 hard-boiled eggs, chopped
15ml/1 tbsp chopped fresh parsley
juice of 2 lemons

Pike with Hard-boiled Eggs
Szczupak po polsku

This dish of poached pike with hard-boiled eggs and parsley is a traditional part of the Christmas Eve meal, although it is eaten at other times of the year too.

VARIATION

If you are unable to buy carp, use river trout instead.

1 Put the carrots in a large pan and add the parsnips, celery, leek, onion, peppercorns, bay leaves and fish.

2 Pour over enough cold water to cover. Bring to the boil and simmer, uncovered, for 15–20 minutes, or until the fish flakes easily.

3 Meanwhile, melt the butter in a small pan, then add the chopped hard-boiled eggs and parsley, and heat through.

4 Remove the fish from the pan with a slotted spoon and transfer to a warm serving plate.

5 Liberally sprinkle the fish with the lemon juice, then pour over the hot hard-boiled egg and parsley mixture and serve immediately.

COOK'S TIP

The addition of egg makes this a nourishing and sustaining dish, perfect for cold weather.

PER SERVING: Energy 327kcal/1368kJ; Protein 39.8g; Carbohydrate 0.2g, of which sugars 0.1g; Fat 18.8g, of which saturates 6.2g; Cholesterol 290mg; Calcium 124mg; Fibre 0.2g; Sodium 178mg.

Serves 4

1 carp, about 900g/2lb, cleaned and filleted
2.5ml/½ tsp salt
50g/2oz/½ cup plain (all-purpose) flour
pinch ground black pepper
1–2 eggs, lightly beaten
115g/4oz/1¾ cups dry breadcrumbs
90ml/6 tbsp vegetable oil, for frying
lemon wedges, to serve

Fried Carp in Breadcrumbs
Karp smażony

This farmhouse dish is the main course of the traditional 12-course Christmas Eve feast, but it makes a delicious meal at any time of the year. Chunks of carp are coated in breadcrumbs and fried in oil, and served simply with lemon wedges.

1 First scald the carp by putting it into a large heatproof dish or roasting pan and pouring boiling water over it. Turn and repeat on the other side. Drain.

2 Cut the cleaned and scalded carp into even-sized portions and sprinkle lightly with salt. Leave to stand for about 30 minutes. Remove the skin, if you like.

3 Mix together the flour and pepper in a medium bowl. Put the beaten egg in another, and the breadcrumbs in a third.

4 Dip the fish pieces first into the flour, then into the egg, then into the breadcrumbs, coating them evenly at each stage.

5 Heat the oil in a large, heavy pan, until very hot. Carefully add the coated fish pieces and cook for about 5 minutes on each side, until golden brown all over.

6 Remove the fish pieces using a slotted spoon and drain on kitchen paper. Serve with lemon wedges.

PER SERVING: Energy 479kcal/2008kJ; Protein 32.3g; Carbohydrate 32g, of which sugars 0.9g; Fat 25.6g, of which saturates 4.1g; Cholesterol 148mg; Calcium 133mg; Fibre 1g; Sodium 301mg.

Serves 4

750ml/1¼ pints/3 cups cold water
120ml/4fl oz/½ cup vinegar
1 medium carp, about 400g/14oz,
   cut into 4 fillets
115g/4oz/1 cup plain (all-purpose) flour
115g/4oz/½ cup butter
250ml/8fl oz/1 cup dry white wine
30ml/2 tbsp grated fresh horseradish
2 egg yolks, beaten
30ml/2 tbsp chopped fresh chives
salt and ground black pepper,
   to taste

COOK'S TIP
Some fish caught in lakes, ponds and rivers
can have a muddy taste, so require soaking in
water and vinegar before use.

Carp with Horseradish Sauce
Karp w sosie chrzanowym

Carp is a traditional fish on Polish menus, and has been
bred since the 13th century. There are several varieties,
the best being the mirror or king carp.

1 Mix the water and vinegar in a
bowl, then soak the carp in the liquid
for 1 hour.

2 Pat dry on kitchen paper, then coat
the fish in flour.

3 Melt the butter over a high heat,
add the fish and fry for 3–4 minutes
on each side, until golden brown.

4 Add the wine and season, then
cover and simmer for 10–15 minutes.

5 Transfer the fish to a serving dish
and keep warm.

6 Add the horseradish and egg yolks
to the juices in the pan and simmer
for 5 minutes, or until thickened.

7 Pour the sauce over the warm fish
and garnish with chopped chives.
Serve immediately.

VARIATION
If you are unable to buy carp, use river
trout instead.

PER SERVING: Energy 500kcal/2083kJ; Protein 22.3g; Carbohydrate 23.2g, of which sugars 1.3g; Fat 31.6g, of which saturates 16.7g; Cholesterol 229mg; Calcium 135mg; Fibre 1.5g; Sodium 229mg.

Serves 4–6

400g/14oz carp, cut into thick portions
750ml/1¼ pints/3 cups water
350ml/12fl oz/1½ cups red wine
30ml/2 tbsp lemon juice
1 small celeriac, sliced
2 onions, sliced
6–8 black peppercorns
2.5ml/½ tsp ground ginger
grated rind of 1 lemon
salt and ground black pepper, to taste

For the sauce
15ml/1 tbsp butter
15ml/1 tbsp plain (all-purpose) flour
45ml/3 tbsp lemon juice
15ml/1 tbsp redcurrant jelly
15ml/1 tbsp clear honey
120ml/4fl oz/½ cup red wine
30ml/2 tbsp currants
30ml/2 tbsp chopped blanched almonds

Carp in Wine Sauce
Karp w sosie ciemnym

This Old Polish carp dish from Krakow forms part of the Christmas Eve meal. Traditionally, the carp was killed and the blood collected in a cup containing lemon juice. This was then added to the sauce. The following version does not require you to do this!

1 Rinse the fish pieces, then sprinkle with salt and leave in a cool place for 20 minutes.

2 Meanwhile, make the stock. Put the water, wine, lemon juice, celeriac, onions, peppercorns, ginger, seasoning and lemon rind in a large pan. Bring to the boil and simmer, uncovered, for 15 minutes. Leave to cool.

3 Place the fish in a shallow pan and pour over the stock and vegetables. Simmer, uncovered, over a low heat for about 15 minutes, or until the fish flakes easily.

4 Remove the fish to a serving plate using a slotted spoon, and keep warm.

5 Skim out the vegetables and press through a fine sieve to form a purée. Add the purée to the stock in the pan. You should have 500ml/17fl oz/2¼ cups stock. Add more water to make up the volume if necessary.

6 To make the sauce, melt the butter in a pan over a medium heat, then add the flour and cook, stirring, for 2 minutes. Stir in the stock.

7 Add the lemon juice, redcurrant jelly, honey and red wine, and cook for 7 minutes.

8 Stir in the currants and almonds, then bring to the boil. Pour the sauce over the carp and serve immediately.

PER SERVING: Energy 213kcal/891kJ; Protein 13.2g; Carbohydrate 9.5g, of which sugars 7.5g; Fat 8g, of which saturates 2.1g; Cholesterol 50mg; Calcium 58mg; Fibre 0.6g; Sodium 52mg.

POULTRY
AND GAME

Potted Goose

Chicken Casserole

Stuffed Roast Turkey

Roast Partridges with Sage,
Thyme and Garlic

Roasted Pheasants

Roast Duck with Fruit Stuffing

Wild Boar with
Sweet-and-sour Sauce

Venison with Wine Sauce

Marinated Hare

Marinated and roasted

Poland is a superb hunting country. Its relatively sparsely populated countryside is covered with forests and fields, where hare, deer, wild boar and many game birds flourish and are now also bred specially for the hunters' guns. Most game needs to be hung for days or even weeks to develop its rich flavour, and before cooking it is usually marinated to add spice to the meat. All the most traditional ingredients of Polish cooking feature in their recipes for game, from juniper berries and herbs to sour cream and mushrooms.

Poultry has a good flavour in Poland, as factory farming is rare and chicken, geese and ducks are instead allowed to roam around on rural smallholdings, eating their natural diet. They are often cooked with a sharp stuffing to cut the richness of the meat, as in Roast Duck with Fruit Stuffing (*Kaczka z owocami*).

Serves 6

5kg/11lb goose, boned and fat reserved
   (ask your butcher to do this or see
   Cook's Tip)
5ml/1 tsp salt
5ml/1 tsp fresh thyme leaves
5ml/1 tsp chopped fresh dill
4 bay leaves
5ml/1 tsp ground allspice
toasted rye bread, to serve

COOK'S TIPS
• It is very easy to remove the bones from the goose yourself, if you prefer. Once the goose portions have been marinated, drain them and pick out the bones with your fingers.
• The potted goose will keep for a couple of months if stored in a dark, cool place.

Potted Goose
Gęś w smalcu

During the summer, many Polish cooks prepare food for the winter. Techniques include pickling, sousing and, as here, sealing goose meat in fat in an airtight container.

1 Cut the goose into large pieces and place in a large bowl.

2 Sprinkle over the salt, thyme, dill, bay leaves and allspice. Toss to coat the meat, then cover, place in the refrigerator and leave to marinate for 48 hours.

3 Place the reserved goose fat in a large pan with a lid and melt gently.

4 Add the goose portions to the pan, cover and simmer very gently for 2–3 hours.

5 Remove the meat with a slotted spoon, then pour a layer of fat into the bottom of a 2 litre/3½ pint/8 cup stoneware pot or preserving jar.

6 Place the goose portions on top of the layer of fat, then pour in enough fat to fill the jar completely.

7 Seal and keep in a cool, dark place until required.

8 Remove the goose from the jar and heat through before serving with toasted rye bread.

PER SERVING: Energy 903kcal/3735kJ; Protein 41.3g; Carbohydrate 0g, of which sugars 0g; Fat 82g, of which saturates 23.8g; Cholesterol 200mg; Calcium 18mg; Fibre 0g; Sodium 153mg.

Chicken Casserole
Potrawka z kurczaka

Warming and nourishing, this casserole is ideal comfort food during cold weather. Served with Buckwheat Kasha it makes a delicious and sustaining main meal.

Serves 4

50g/2oz dried mushrooms, rinsed and
   soaked in warm water for 30 minutes
800g/1¾lb chicken pieces
550ml/18fl oz/2½ cups water
2 celery stalks, chopped
1 carrot, chopped
30ml/2 tbsp chopped fresh parsley
25g/1oz/2 tbsp butter
25g/1oz/2 tbsp plain (all-purpose) flour
120ml/4fl oz/½ cup dry white wine
2 egg yolks
salt and ground black pepper, to taste
Buckwheat Kasha (see page 94),
   to serve

COOK'S TIP
To get the full, authentic flavour of this traditional casserole, it's best to use organic chicken.

1 Strain the mushrooms, reserving the juices, then chop finely. Put the chicken in a flameproof casserole, add the water and bring to the boil. Simmer for 10 minutes.

2 Add the mushrooms, celery, carrot, parsley and reserved mushroom juices to the casserole. Season, then cover and simmer for 30–45 minutes.

3 Meanwhile, make the roux. Melt the butter in a small pan, add the flour and cook, stirring, for 1 minute.

4 Remove the chicken from the casserole with a slotted spoon and set aside on a warm plate. Add the roux to the casserole and stir. Add the wine and bring to the boil.

5 Remove the casserole from the heat. Put the egg yolks in a small bowl and add a ladleful of the hot juices, stirring constantly. Add to the casserole and stir to combine.

6 Return the chicken to the sauce and heat gently to warm through. Serve with Buckwheat Kasha.

PER SERVING: Energy 285kcal/1196kJ; Protein 38.3g; Carbohydrate 6.7g, of which sugars 1.8g; Fat 9.7g, of which saturates 4.5g; Cholesterol 219mg; Calcium 43mg; Fibre 0.8g; Sodium 148mg.

Stuffed Roast Turkey
Nadziewany indyk po polsku

Turkey is one of the cheaper types of poultry in Poland and is often used to replace more expensive goose. It is best to buy birds that are between seven and nine months old. In this simple recipe the bird is stuffed with a rich herb stuffing and served with cranberry jelly.

Serves 6

1 turkey, about 4.5–5.5kg/10–12lb, washed and patted dry with kitchen paper
25g/1oz/2 tbsp butter, melted
salt and ground black pepper, to taste
cranberry jelly, to serve

For the stuffing

200g/7oz/3½ cups fresh white breadcrumbs
175ml/6fl oz/¾ cup milk
25g/1oz/2 tbsp butter
1 egg, separated
1 calf's liver, about 600g/1lb 6oz, finely chopped
2 onions, finely chopped
90ml/6 tbsp chopped fresh dill
10ml/2 tsp clear honey
salt and ground black pepper, to taste

1 To make the stuffing, put the breadcrumbs and milk in a large bowl and soak until swollen and soft. Melt the butter in a frying pan and mix 5ml/1 tsp with the egg yolk.

2 Heat the remaining butter in a frying pan and add the liver and onions. Fry gently for 5 minutes, until the onions are golden brown. Remove from the heat and leave to cool.

3 Preheat the oven to 180°C/350°F/Gas 4. Add the cooled liver mixture to the soaked breadcrumbs and add the butter and egg yolk mixture, with the dill, honey and seasoning.

4 Whisk the egg white to soft peaks then fold into the mixture, stirring gently to combine thoroughly.

5 Season the turkey inside and out with salt and pepper. Stuff the cavity with the stuffing mixture, then weigh to calculate the cooking time. Allow 20 minutes per 500g/1¼lb, plus an additional 20 minutes. Tuck the legs inside the cavity and tie the end shut with string.

6 Brush the outside with melted butter and transfer to a roasting pan. Place in the oven and roast for the calculated time.

7 Baste the turkey regularly during cooking, and cover with foil for the final 30 minutes if the skin becomes too brown. To test whether the turkey is cooked, pierce the thickest part of the thigh with a knife; the juices should run clear.

8 Remove the turkey from the oven, cover with foil and leave to rest for about 15 minutes. Carve into thin slices, then spoon over the juices and serve with the stuffing and cranberry jelly.

PER SERVING: Energy 740kcal/3126kJ; Protein 112.3g; Carbohydrate 35.9g, of which sugars 7.3g; Fat 13.5g, of which saturates 6.6g; Cholesterol 507mg; Calcium 122mg; Fibre 1.7g; Sodium 517mg.

Serves 4

4 small partridges, cleaned and gutted
8 slices pork fat or streaky (fatty) bacon
50g/2oz/¼ cup butter, softened, plus
  5ml/3 tbsp melted butter, for basting
10 fresh sage leaves, roughly chopped
1 bunch fresh thyme, leaves chopped
10 garlic cloves, roughly chopped
salt and ground black pepper, to taste
cranberry preserve,
  to serve (optional)

Roast Partridges with Sage, Thyme and Garlic
Pieczone kuropatwy przepiórki

It is important that you select young birds for this simple recipe. Basting the meat regularly during the cooking time prevents the flesh from drying out and adds a lovely buttery flavour, and the herbs and garlic add a subtle yet distinctive note.

1 Preheat the oven to 190°C/375°F/ Gas 5. Season the partridges well inside and out, then place in a roasting pan.

2 Lay the slices of pork fat or bacon over the birds.

3 Mix together the softened butter, herbs and garlic, and use to stuff the cavities of the birds.

4 Place in the oven and roast for about 1½ hours, until cooked through, basting often with the butter.

5 Remove from the oven, cover with foil and allow to rest for 15 minutes.

6 Serve with cranberry preserve, if you like.

COOK'S TIP
To test if they are cooked, pierce the thickest part of the thigh; the juices should run clear.

PER SERVING: Energy 866kcal/3619kJ; Protein 118g; Carbohydrate 0.1g, of which sugars 0.1g; Fat 43.6g, of which saturates 16.1g; Cholesterol 59mg; Calcium 145mg; Fibre 0g; Sodium 1006mg.

Serves 4

2 medium-sized pheasants,
  cleaned and gutted (ask your
  butcher to do this)
150g/5oz streaky (fatty) bacon, cut into
  thin strips
4–5 dried mushrooms, rinsed and
  soaked in warm water for
  30 minutes
150g/5oz/10 tbsp butter, melted
15ml/1 tbsp plain (all-purpose) flour
300ml/½ pint/1¼ cups sour cream
salt and ground black pepper,
  to taste
Beetroot Salad (see page 97),
  to serve

For the marinade

175ml/6fl oz/¾ cup dry white wine
200ml/7fl oz/scant 1 cup water
90ml/6 tbsp vinegar
1 large onion, roughly chopped
1 carrot, roughly chopped
½ celeriac, roughly chopped
1 parsnip, roughly chopped
5–8 juniper berries, crushed
4 bay leaves
6 allspice berries
6 whole cloves
5ml/1 tsp sugar
salt and ground black pepper,
  to taste

Roasted Pheasants
Bażant w sosie kremowym

Juniper berries, allspice, cloves and bay leaves are the
key components of the marinade for this delicious dish.
Long marinating ensures the flavours permeate the flesh.

1 To make the marinade, put all the
ingredients in a large pan and bring
to the boil.

2 Place the pheasants in a large dish
or stainless steel pan and pour over
the marinade. Cover and leave to
cool, then place in the refrigerator
and leave to marinate for 2–3 days,
turning the pheasants occasionally.

3 Preheat the oven to 220°C/425°F/
Gas 7. Lift out the pheasants and
season all over.

4 Place in a roasting pan with the
vegetables from the marinade. Roll
up the bacon strips and place inside
the cavities.

5 Drain and chop the mushrooms.
Pour the melted butter all over
the pheasants and sprinkle the
mushrooms over the top.

6 Place in the oven and roast for
about 1 hour. To test whether they are
cooked, pierce the thickest part with
a knife; the juices should run clear.

7 Mix the flour with the sour cream,
then pour over the pheasants. Cover
with foil and cook for a further 10
minutes, or until the sauce is thick.

8 Remove from the oven and leave to
rest for 15 minutes. Remove the foil,
carve, then serve with the vegetables,
sauce and Beetroot Salad.

PER SERVING: Energy 1114kcal/4636kJ; Protein 89.9g; Carbohydrate 6.3g, of which sugars 3.4g; Fat 78.3g, of which saturates 40g; Cholesterol 149mg; Calcium 212mg; Fibre 0.1g; Sodium 996mg.

Serves 4
1 large duck, about 2.75kg/6lb
3 apples, chopped
2 whole oranges, chopped
12 prunes, chopped
12 fresh or dried apricots, chopped
175ml/6fl oz/¾ cup fresh orange juice
30ml/2 tbsp clear honey
Spiced Red Cabbage (see page 87),
  to serve

For the marinade
juice of 1 lemon
5ml/1 tsp dried marjoram
salt and ground black pepper, to taste

COOK'S TIP
Duck is a fatty bird, so it is best roasted with a stuffing that will cut the fat, such as this fresh, fruity one.

Roast Duck with Fruit Stuffing
Kaczka z owocami

Duck is considered a luxury in Poland, and is usually reserved for special occasions. Often, as in this recipe, it is roasted and served with a range of different fruits.

1 Wash the duck and pat dry with kitchen paper, then put it into a large dish.

2 Mix the marinade ingredients together in a small bowl, then rub over the duck. Cover and leave to marinate for 2 hours, or overnight.

3 Preheat the oven to 180°C/350°F/ Gas 4. Mix together the apples, oranges, prunes, apricots, orange juice and honey, then stuff into the cavity.

4 Weigh the duck and calculate the cooking time: allow 20 minutes per 500g/1¼lb, plus an extra 20 minutes.

5 Place the duck in a roasting pan and roast for the calculated time. To test whether it is cooked, pierce the thickest part with a knife; the juices should run clear.

6 Cover with foil and allow it to rest for about 15 minutes. Remove the fruit from the cavity and carve the meat.

7 Transfer the meat to a serving platter and arrange the fruit around it. Serve with Spiced Red Cabbage.

PER SERVING: Energy 468kcal/1983kJ; Protein 43.5g; Carbohydrate 54.1g, of which sugars 54.1g; Fat 13.7g, of which saturates 2.6g; Cholesterol 220mg; Calcium 99mg; Fibre 7.8g; Sodium 241mg.

Serves 4–6

1 piece wild boar rump,
  about 2kg/4½lb
115g/4oz/⅔ cup lard
30ml/2 tbsp plain (all-purpose) flour
15ml/1 tbsp rosehip preserve
5ml/1 tsp ground cinnamon
5ml/1 tsp sugar
5ml/1 tsp salt
redcurrant jelly, to serve

For the marinade
500ml/17fl oz/2¼ cups water
500ml/17fl oz/2¼ cups dry red wine
90ml/6 tbsp vinegar
2 strips of lemon rind
2 onions, sliced
3 large garlic cloves, chopped
1 carrot, chopped
½ celeriac, chopped
1 parsnip, chopped
15 prunes
10 black peppercorns
10 allspice berries, cracked
4–5 whole cloves
20 juniper berries
4 bay leaves
1 piece fresh root ginger, chopped

Wild Boar with Sweet-and-sour Sauce
Cząber z dzika

Harking back to ancient days when hunters caught wild boar in the forests around
Poland, this Old Polish recipe involves marinating the tender rump for several days
before roasting and serving it with a flavoursome sauce.

1 Place all the marinade ingredients
in a stainless steel pan and bring to
the boil. Simmer for 5 minutes, then
cool. Add the meat, cover and chill.
Leave to marinate for 3–4 days.

2 Preheat the oven to 180°C/350°F/
Gas 4. Heat the lard in a flameproof
casserole. Add the meat and brown
all over. Scoop out the vegetables and
lemon from the marinade and add to
the meat in the casserole.

3 Strain the marinade. Add to the
casserole. Cook for 2 hours. Lift out
the meat, cover and rest for 15 minutes.

4 Mix together the flour, rosehip
preserve, cinnamon, sugar and salt,
then add to the casserole. Stir to mix
and return to the oven for 10 minutes.

5 Carve the meat into slices, then
transfer to plates and spoon over the
sauce. Serve with redcurrant jelly.

PER SERVING: Energy 655kcal/2734kJ; Protein 73g; Carbohydrate 17.4g, of which sugars 8.8g; Fat 33g, of which saturates 12.5g; Cholesterol 228mg; Calcium 63mg; Fibre 3.3g; Sodium 578mg.

Serves 4

100g/3½oz fresh wild mushrooms,
   cut in half
4 venison loin steaks, 2cm/¾in thick
25g/1oz/¼ cup plain (all-purpose) flour
25g/1oz/2 tbsp butter
1 large onion, sliced into rings
5ml/1 tsp fresh thyme leaves
5ml/1 tsp juniper berries
5–6 allspice berries
5 bay leaves
4 garlic cloves, crushed
175ml/6fl oz/¾ cup white wine
salt and ground black pepper, to taste

COOK'S TIP
Wild boar and venison used to be the
staple foods in Poland in ancient times.
Although eaten less frequently, they are
both still enjoyed today.

Venison with Wine Sauce
Jeleń w sosie winnym

Tender venison steaks are the perfect partner to the wild
mushrooms that abound in Poland's forests. Here they
are cooked simply and served with a rich wine sauce.

1 Brush the mushrooms to remove
any grit, and wash the caps briefly if
necessary. Dry with kitchen paper.

2 Lightly dust the venison steaks with
the flour.

3 Heat the butter in a heavy pan with
a lid, then add the onion rings and
venison, and fry for 5 minutes, until
the onions have softened and the
steaks are brown on both sides.

4 Add the remaining ingredients to
the pan and season to taste. Cover
and simmer for 30 minutes.

5 Taste and adjust the seasoning,
if necessary. Transfer to plates and
serve immediately.

PER SERVING: Energy 303kcal/1276kJ; Protein 45.1g; Carbohydrate 5.2g, of which sugars 0.4g; Fat 9.6g, of which saturates 4.9g; Cholesterol 113mg; Calcium 24mg; Fibre 0.2g; Sodium 150mg.

Serves 4

saddle and thighs of 1 hare
120ml/4fl oz/½ cup vinegar
900ml/1½ pints/3¾ cups buttermilk
175g/6oz/¾ cup butter
5 large dried mushrooms, rinsed and
   soaked in warm water for 30 minutes,
   thinly sliced
15ml/1 tbsp plain (all-purpose) flour
200ml/7fl oz/scant 1 cup thick
   sour cream
175ml/6fl oz/¾ cup white wine
salt and ground black pepper,
   to taste
cranberry preserve, to serve (optional)

For the marinade:

10–15 juniper berries
2 large onions, cut into slices
½ celeriac, chopped
2 parsnips, chopped
2 carrots, chopped
3 large garlic cloves, crushed
5 bay leaves

COOK'S TIP

An important part of Polish cuisine
involves marinating game before it is
cooked. This process helps to tenderize
the meat and also adds flavour to the
finished dish.

Marinated Hare
Zając w sosie

In this delectable dish, the saddle and thighs of a hare are
marinated in buttermilk and vegetables, before being
roasted and then baked with a cream sauce.

1 Place the hare pieces, vinegar and all the marinade ingredients in a large dish and pour in enough buttermilk to cover.

2 Add salt and pepper, cover with clear film (plastic wrap) and place in the refrigerator.

3 Leave to marinate for 2–3 days, changing the buttermilk after the first day.

4 Drain off the marinade and buttermilk. Preheat the oven to 180°C/350°F/Gas 4.

5 Transfer the hare pieces to a roasting pan, rub with 15ml/1 tbsp salt, and dot with the butter.

6 Slice the mushrooms and sprinkle over the hare.

7 Cover and roast for 1–1½ hours, or until cooked through.

8 Mix the flour with the sour cream and white wine, then add to the roasting pan.

9 Cover the pan with foil and replace in the oven. Cook for a further 15–20 minutes, or until the sauce is thick and bubbling.

10 Transfer to a warm serving dish and spoon over the creamy sauce.

11 Serve immediately, with cranberry preserve, if you like.

PER SERVING: Energy 581kcal/2423kJ; Protein 62.9g; Carbohydrate 6.9g, of which sugars 3g; Fat 29.5g, of which saturates 8.4g; Cholesterol 40mg; Calcium 118mg; Fibre 0.5g; Sodium 111mg.

MEAT

Roast Lamb with Garlic,
Rosemary and Thyme

Roast Fillet of Pork
with Prunes

Breaded Pork Cutlets

Pork Rib Stew with Cabbage

Hunter's Stew

Stuffed Cabbage Rolls

Veal Stroganoff

Roast Beef Roll

Fried Calf's Brains

Krakow-style Calf's Liver

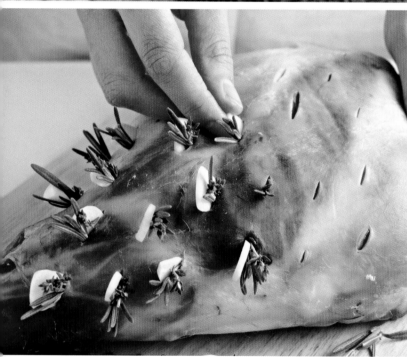

Hearty and tender

Even though meat can be expensive in Poland, it is still a staple of the Polish diet. All kinds of meat are eaten, cooked in all sorts of ways, from quick pan-fried dishes, such as breaded veal or Breaded Pork Cutlets *(Kotlet schabowy)*, simple roast joints flavoured with herbs, and Hunter's Stew *(Bigos)*, which is reheated two or even three times in order to intensify the flavours.

Poland's rural population developed many recipes for using all parts of the animal, including the offal, which is a highly prized delicacy often eaten as a snack, on toast. Cheaper cuts take longer to cook, and the more traditional recipes involving slowly cooked meat in stock with vegetables, such as Pork Rib Stew with Cabbage *(Żeberka wieprzowe)*, would have been found simmering on many cottage stoves during the winter months.

Serves 6

2kg/4½lb leg of lamb
fresh rosemary, separated
  into sprigs
fresh thyme, separated into sprigs
10 garlic cloves, cut into slivers
5ml/1 tsp black peppercorns
6 whole cloves
6 allspice berries
20g/¾oz butter, softened
redcurrant jelly, to serve

Roast Lamb with Garlic, Rosemary and Thyme
Noga jagnięcia z ziołami

Simply roasting lamb with a selection of aromatic ingredients brings out the best in the meat. In this delicious recipe the lamb is rubbed with a mixture of butter, pepper, cloves and allspice, which lend a distinctive spicy Polish note to the meat.

1 Preheat the oven to 200°C/400°F/ Gas 6. Place the leg of lamb in a roasting pan.

2 Make about 20–30 small, deep slits all over the meat, then push a small sprig of rosemary and thyme and a sliver of garlic into each.

3 Using a pestle and mortar, grind the peppercorns, cloves and allspice to a coarse powder. Combine the powder with the softened butter and smear all over the lamb.

4 Place the roasting pan in the hot oven and cook for 15 minutes. Reduce the heat to 180°C/350°F/ Gas 4 and roast the lamb for a further 1½ hours, or until cooked but still slightly pink.

5 Remove the joint from the oven, cover with foil and allow it to rest for 15 minutes.

6 Cut the meat into generous slices and serve immediately with redcurrant jelly.

PER SERVING: Energy 562kcal/2340kJ; Protein 50.4g; Carbohydrate 0.4g, of which sugars 0.3g; Fat 39.9g, of which saturates 14.1g; Cholesterol 200mg; Calcium 36mg; Fibre 0.6g; Sodium 171mg.

Serves 4–6
1.8kg/4lb pork fillet (tenderloin)
2.5ml/½ tsp dried marjoram
15ml/1 tbsp caraway seeds
4–5 bay leaves
90ml/6 tbsp white wine
30ml/2 tbsp vegetable oil
225g/8oz ready-to-eat prunes, chopped
salt and ground black pepper, to taste
lettuce and Beetroot Salad (see page 97),
to serve

Roast Fillet of Pork with Prunes
Wieprzowina ze suszonymi śliwkami

Pork is the national meat of Poland, and this recipe of roasted marinated pork fillet stuffed with prunes is a wonderful example of how its delectable flavour can be fully appreciated. Serve with salads for a light lunch, or with Buckwheat Kasha for a more sustaining meal.

1 Partially cut the fillet lengthways leaving one long side attached. Rub with salt, pepper and marjoram, then sprinkle with caraway seeds. Put into a dish and add the bay leaves, then pour over the wine. Cover and leave to marinate for about 2 hours.

2 Preheat the oven to 180°C/350°F/ Gas 4. Pour the oil into a roasting pan and put in the oven to heat.

3 Take the pork fillet out of the marinade and lay the chopped prunes along half of the opened-out fillet. Fold the top half over and tie the fillet together using string.

4 Place in the hot oil and put into the oven. Roast for about 1½ hours, or until the meat is cooked, basting occasionally with the meat juices.

5 Remove the meat from the oven and allow to rest, covered in foil, for 15 minutes. Remove the string and cut into slices. Spoon over the cooking juices and serve immediately with lettuce and Beetroot Salad.

PER SERVING: Energy 537kcal/2247kJ; Protein 63.1g; Carbohydrate 12.8g, of which sugars 12.8g; Fat 15.8g, of which saturates 7.9g; Cholesterol 207mg; Calcium 38mg; Fibre 2.1g; Sodium 233mg.

Serves 4

4 boneless pork cutlets, fat on,
  each weighing about 225g/8oz
2.5ml/½ tsp salt
2.5ml/½ tsp ground black pepper
115g/4oz/1 cup plain (all-purpose) flour
2 eggs, beaten
65g/2½oz/1 cup fine fresh breadcrumbs
1 tbsp each of chopped fresh rosemary,
  dill and sage
75ml/5 tbsp vegetable oil
fresh parsley sprigs, to garnish
lemon wedges, mashed potato and
  sauerkraut or red cabbage,
  to serve

Breaded Pork Cutlets
Kotlet schabowy

Easy to make and quick to cook, this recipe for pork cutlets dipped in breadcrumbs and simply fried is particularly popular in Poland.

COOK'S TIP

It is important that you serve the cutlets immediately as they will become tough if they are left to stand.

1 Cut slits in the rind of the pork cutlets to prevent it from curling during cooking. Using a meat mallet, rolling pin or the base of a frying pan, pound each cutlet lightly on each side to flatten, then sprinkle each side with salt and pepper.

2 Put the flour and beaten eggs in separate bowls. In another bowl, mix the breadcrumbs with the chopped herbs.

3 Dip the cutlets first in the flour, then the egg and then into the breadcrumb mixture.

4 Heat the oil in a frying pan, then add the breaded pork and fry on a high heat for 4–5 minutes on each side, until golden brown all over.

5 Reduce the heat and cook for a further 2 minutes to ensure the pork is cooked all the way through.

6 Garnish with parsley and serve immediately with mashed potato and sauerkraut or red cabbage, and with lemon wedges for squeezing over.

PER SERVING: Energy 591kcal/2475kJ; Protein 55.9g; Carbohydrate 34.9g, of which sugars 0.9g; Fat 26.2g, of which saturates 5.6g; Cholesterol 237mg; Calcium 92mg; Fibre 1.3g; Sodium 317mg.

Pork Rib Stew with Cabbage
Żeberka wieprzowe

This delicious stew makes the most of cheap ingredients, combining flavoursome ribs with a simple broth and some fresh green cabbage.

Serves 4–6

40g/1½oz/¼ cup bacon dripping or
 40ml/2½ tbsp vegetable oil
1.8kg/4lb pork spare ribs
900ml/1½ pints/3¾ cups beef stock
6 black peppercorns
4 bay leaves
5ml/1 tsp caraway seeds
5ml/1 tsp paprika
2 large onions, roughly chopped
2–3 carrots, roughly chopped
3–4 garlic cloves, roughly chopped
175ml/6fl oz/¾ cup dry white wine
1 cabbage, quartered and
 core removed
chopped fresh parsley or dill,
 to garnish
boiled new potatoes, to serve

1 Heat the bacon dripping or oil in a heavy pan, add the spare ribs and cook over a high heat for 5 minutes, or until brown all over.

2 Add the stock, peppercorns, bay leaves, caraway seeds, paprika, onions, carrots, garlic and white wine. Cover the pan and simmer over a low heat for about 1½ hours.

3 Add the cabbage and cook for a further 30 minutes, until tender.

4 Ladle on to plates, garnish with parsley or dill and serve immediately with boiled new potatoes.

PER SERVING: Energy 539kcal/2241kJ; Protein 45g; Carbohydrate 6.1g, of which sugars 5.9g; Fat 35.1g, of which saturates 11.2g; Cholesterol 159mg; Calcium 62mg; Fibre 2.2g; Sodium 161mg.

Hunter's Stew
Bigos

Considered by some to be the national dish, *bigos* is one of the most treasured of the Old Polish recipes. Hearty and sustaining, this sauerkraut, cabbage and meat stew can be found in many different forms throughout the country, depending on what is available and individual preference. It is usually allowed to cool and then reheated several times so that the flavours can intensify, and it is often served with rye bread to mop up the delicious juices, and vodka – said to aid digestion. Start preparing it a day in advance.

Serves 6–8

1kg/2¼ lb fresh cabbage, finely shredded
10 dried mushrooms (boletus)
2 onions, chopped
500g/1¼ lb smoked sausage, sliced
1kg/2¼ lb sauerkraut, drained
2 cooking apples, peeled, cored
   and diced
10 prunes
10 juniper berries, crushed
3–4 bay leaves
10 peppercorns
2.5ml/½ tsp salt
750ml/1¼ pints/3 cups boiling water
500g/1¼ lb roast pork, diced
500g/1¼ lb roast beef, diced
500g/1¼lb boiled ham, diced
150ml/¼ pint/⅔ cup dry red wine
5ml/1 tsp honey
wholemeal (whole-wheat) or rye bread
   and chilled vodka, to serve

COOK'S TIP
The more times you cool and reheat the stew, the better the flavour will become. Make sure it is brought to the boil and thoroughly simmered before serving.

1 Place the cabbage in a heatproof colander and wilt the leaves by carefully pouring boiling water over it.

2 Rinse the mushrooms, then place them in a bowl with enough warm water to cover. Leave to soak for 15 minutes, then transfer to a pan and cook in the soaking liquid for 30 minutes. Strain, reserving the cooking liquid, then cut the mushrooms into strips.

3 Put the onions and smoked sausage in a small frying pan and fry gently, until the onions have softened. Remove the sausage from the pan and set aside.

4 Put the wilted cabbage and drained sauerkraut in a large pan, then add the cooked onions, along with the mushrooms, mushroom cooking liquid, apples, prunes, juniper berries, bay leaves, peppercorns and salt. Pour over the boiling water, then cover and simmer gently for 1 hour.

5 Add the cooked sausage to the pan with the other cooked, diced meats. Pour in the wine and add the honey.

6 Cook, uncovered, for a further 40 minutes, stirring frequently. Taste and adjust the seasoning as required. Remove from the heat.

7 Allow the stew to cool, then cover it and transfer to the refrigerator. Leave it overnight. Return to the boil and simmer for 10 minutes to heat through. Serve with wholemeal or rye bread and a glass of chilled vodka.

VARIATION Any leftover meat, such as duck, lamb or venison, works well in this stew.

PER SERVING: 546kcal/2279kJ; Protein 50.4g; Carbohydrate 24.6g, of which sugars 19.8g; Fat 26.4g, of which saturates 9.7g; Cholesterol 149mg; Calcium 213mg; Fibre 7.7g; Sodium 2122mg.

Stuffed Cabbage Rolls
Gołąbki

Gołąbki, meaning "little pigeons", are one of the most popular dishes in Poland. Simple to prepare, cheap and very tasty, they can be made ahead in large quantities and reheated, since the flavour improves with age. If you have any stuffing mixture left over, freeze it until required, then simply defrost and use to stuff more leaves.

Serves 4
1 small cabbage
1 small (US medium) egg, beaten
2.5ml/½ tsp freshly grated nutmeg
10ml/2 tsp chopped fresh parsley
10ml/2 tsp vegetable oil
400g/14oz can chopped tomatoes
60ml/4 tbsp boiling water
salt and ground black pepper, to taste

For the stuffing
100g/3¾oz/½ cup long grain rice
15g/½oz/¼ cup dried wild mushrooms, rinsed and soaked in warm water for 30 minutes
15ml/1 tbsp butter
½ large onion, finely chopped
225g/8oz/1 cup minced (ground) pork
225g/8oz/1 cup minced (ground) beef
1 garlic clove, finely chopped

VARIATIONS
• Instead of baking the cabbage rolls, you could fry them in pork fat or lard for 10–15 minutes.
• Replace the rice with an equal amount of cooked buckwheat, if you like.
• A vegetarian version of these rolls, made with mushrooms in place of the meat, is sometimes served as part of the Christmas Eve feast.

1 To make the stuffing, bring a large pan of lightly salted water to the boil and cook the rice, according to the instructions on the packet. Once the grains are tender, drain and rinse under cold water to prevent them from cooking further.

2 Drain the mushrooms and chop them finely. Heat half the butter in a large pan, then add the onion and fry gently until golden brown.

3 Add the pork, beef, garlic, mushrooms and seasoning. Cook, stirring, until the meat is browned all over, then remove from the heat and leave to cool slightly.

4 Bring a large pan of lightly salted water to the boil and cook the whole cabbage for 10–15 minutes, or until you can insert a knife into the centre easily, but the leaves are not too soft. Lift the cabbage out of the water and leave to cool slightly.

5 Preheat the oven to 190°C/375°F/Gas 5. Add the egg, nutmeg and parsley to the meat mixture and stir to combine well.

6 When it is cool enough to handle, separate the cabbage into individual leaves. Use the tough outside leaves to line an ovenproof dish. Drizzle over the oil.

7 Place a spoonful of the meat mixture in the centre of each of the remaining cabbage leaves, fold over the edges and roll to form a tight package.

8 Arrange the rolls in a single layer on the oiled cabbage leaves in the dish. Pour over the tomatoes and boiling water, and dot the remaining butter over the top. Cover the dish with a lid or foil.

9 Cook in the preheated oven for about 1 hour, or until the rolls are tender. Serve immediately, with spoonfuls of the tomato sauce.

PER SERVING: Energy 414kcal/1725kJ; Protein 27.6g; Carbohydrate 28.7g, of which sugars 8.2g; Fat 21g, of which saturates 8.5g; Cholesterol 126mg; Calcium 99mg; Fibre 3.4g; Sodium 133mg.

Serves 4–6

15g/½oz/2 tbsp plain (all-purpose) flour
2.5ml/½ tsp cayenne pepper
2.5ml/½ tsp hot paprika
900g/2lb veal fillet, cut into fine strips
60ml/4 tbsp vegetable oil
2 small onions, finely chopped
4 garlic cloves, finely chopped
8–10 fresh wild mushrooms,
   wiped clean and halved
150ml/¼ pint/⅔ cup brandy
5ml/1 tsp Polish or Dijon mustard
400ml/14fl oz/1⅔ cups veal or beef stock
400ml/14fl oz/1⅔ cups sour cream
salt and ground black pepper, to taste
30ml/2 tbsp chopped fresh flat leaf
   parsley, to garnish
cooked egg noodles or rice, to serve

COOK'S TIP
So that you can slice the meat very finely, place the veal fillet in the freezer for 30 minutes beforehand.

Veal Stroganoff
Cielęcy stroganoff

"Stroganoff" dishes are thought to have originated in St Petersburg in the 19th century, where the beef dish was created and named after Count Pavel Alexandrovich Stroganov. The recipe was rapidly assimilated into Polish cuisine, and has become a much-loved classic.

1 Mix together the flour, cayenne pepper and paprika in a bowl, and toss the strips of meat in it. Set aside.

2 Heat half the oil in a heavy pan, then add the onions and garlic. Fry gently for 5 minutes, or until soft and brown.

3 Add the mushrooms and fry for a further 5 minutes. Transfer the vegetables to a plate and keep warm.

4 Pour the remaining oil into the frying pan and heat. When the oil is hot, add the floured meat strips and stir-fry over a high heat for about 2 minutes, until the meat is brown.

5 Return the vegetables to the pan and add the brandy, mustard, veal or beef stock and seasoning.

6 Simmer for 1 minute, then add the sour cream. Simmer for 1 minute more, until thick and glossy.

7 Serve immediately, garnished with parsley, with egg noodles or rice.

PER SERVING: Energy 511kcal/2124kJ; Protein 33.7g; Carbohydrate 9.9g, of which sugars 6.3g; Fat 31.6g, of which saturates 13.6g; Cholesterol 133mg; Calcium 97mg; Fibre 1g; Sodium 434mg.

Serves 4–6

1.3kg/3lb piece boneless rump steak
25g/1oz/2 tbsp butter
120ml/4fl oz/½ cup beef stock
pinch of salt
Buckwheat Kasha (see page 94) and a
    green salad or poached beetroots
    (beets), to serve

For the stuffing

50g/2oz/½ cups dried mushrooms,
    soaked in warm water for 30 minutes
25g/1oz streaky (fatty) smoked bacon
15g/½oz/1 tbsp butter
½ onion, finely chopped
15ml/1 tbsp fresh breadcrumbs
1 egg, beaten
15ml/1 tbsp sour cream
15ml/1 tbsp finely chopped fresh parsley
salt and ground black pepper,
    to taste

Roast Beef Roll
Zrazy

This traditional Polish dish is a combination of fine steak
and stong-flavoured mushrooms. Stuffed meat dishes
such as this have been a part of Polish cooking since
the 17th century, and they are usually served on festive
occasions or as part of a special Polish dinner.

1 To make the stuffing, strain the
mushrooms and put into a food
processor with the bacon. Process to
form a paste, then scrape into a bowl.

2 Heat the butter in a pan, then add
the onion and fry for 5 minutes. Leave
to cool, then add to the bowl with the
breadcrumbs, egg, sour cream, parsley
and seasoning. Knead to combine.

3 Using a mallet, pound the steak to
the thickness of your little finger.
Spread the stuffing all over the meat,
then roll tightly. Tuck the edges in and
tie with scalded white cotton thread.

4 Heat the butter in a large pan.
Sprinkle the roll with salt, then add
to the pan and seal on all sides. Add
the stock and simmer for 30 minutes.
Place a roasting pan in the oven and
preheat to 180°C/350°F/Gas 4.

5 Transfer the beef roll and the juices
to the pan and roast for 30 minutes.
Check the meat occasionally and add
more stock if required.

6 Remove the thread and cut into thin
slices. Ladle over the juices and
serve with Buckwheat Kasha and a
green salad in summer or beetroots.

PER SERVING: Energy 360kcal/1510kJ; Protein 50.1g; Carbohydrate 2.9g, of which sugars 0.8g; Fat 16.6g, of which saturates 8g; Cholesterol 177mg; Calcium 23mg; Fibre 0.3g; Sodium 267mg.

Serves 4
675g/1½lb calf's brains
40g/1½oz/3 tbsp butter
1 large onion, finely chopped
2 eggs, beaten
60ml/4 tbsp fresh breadcrumbs
8 slices hot buttered toast
salt and ground black pepper,
   to taste
chopped fresh parsley, to garnish

Fried Calf's Brains
Móżdżek po polsku

Rich, creamy, and nutritious calf's brains are a real treat. In this classic Polish recipe they are fried with onions, eggs and breadcrumbs, and served on toast.

1 Thoroughly rinse the brains under cold running water. Remove the membrane and finely chop.

2 Heat the butter in a large frying pan, add the onion and cook for about 5 minutes, or until golden brown.

3 Add the brains and fry for 5 minutes, stirring, until golden brown.

4 Add the eggs and breadcrumbs and cook for a further 2 minutes, stirring, until the eggs are cooked. Season to taste with salt and pepper.

5 Place the pieces of toast on four serving plates, then top with the hot brain mixture and garnish with chopped parsley.

PER SERVING: Energy 521kcal/2172kJ; Protein 27.1g; Carbohydrate 26.5g, of which sugars 2.1g; Fat 34.9g, of which saturates 14.6g; Cholesterol 3850mg; Calcium 90mg; Fibre 1g; Sodium 768mg.

Krakow-style Calf's Liver
Cielęca wątróbka

Flavoursome and very nutritious, liver is popular all over Poland. In this recipe it is served with a mushroom sauce.

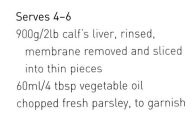

Serves 4–6
900g/2lb calf's liver, rinsed, membrane removed and sliced into thin pieces
60ml/4 tbsp vegetable oil
chopped fresh parsley, to garnish

For the sauce
45ml/3 tbsp butter
1 large onion, sliced
175g/6oz/2½ cups button (white) mushrooms, wiped clean and chopped
15g/½oz/2 tbsp plain (all-purpose) flour
175ml/6fl oz/¾ cup dry white wine
250ml/8fl oz/1 cup sour cream
salt and ground black pepper, to taste

1 To make the sauce, heat the butter in a pan, then add the onion and mushrooms. Cook for 5–8 minutes, or until the onion is softened.

2 Stir in the flour and cook for 1 minute, then add the wine and cook for a further 3 minutes. Add the sour cream and season to taste. Keep the sauce warm, but do not allow it to boil.

3 Sprinkle the liver with pepper. Heat the oil in a frying pan, add the liver and cook for 1–2 minutes on each side, until brown on the outside and pink in the middle.

4 Transfer to serving plates, pour over the sauce and garnish with fresh parsley. Serve immediately.

PER SERVING: Energy 410kcal/1705kJ; Protein 29.5g; Carbohydrate 6g, of which sugars 3g; Fat 27.9g, of which saturates 11.7g; Cholesterol 596mg; Calcium 67mg; Fibre 0.3g; Sodium 288mg.

SIDE DISHES AND SALADS

Sautéed Wild Mushrooms

Spiced Red Cabbage

Grated Potato Dumplings

Mashed Potato Dumplings

Potato and Cheese Dumplings

Dumplings Stuffed with Mushrooms

Buckwheat Kasha

Polish-style Cucumber Salad

Apple and Leek Salad

Beetroot Salad

Zesty and sustaining

Both cold salads and hot side dishes are a common feature of Polish meals. Many, such as Buckwheat Kasha *(Kasza gryczana)*, are made from ingredients that have been grown on the plains of central Poland since the Middle Ages. Strong-tasting buckwheat is highly prized in Poland, and makes a splendid foil for roast meat or, with the addition of honey, a tasty breakfast. Other hot dishes include savoury dumplings, which are often based on potatoes or even a simple flour and water mixture combined with an appetizing filling.

All kinds of salad are eaten throughout the year as an accompaniment to hot and cold main courses. Beetroot Salad *(Ćwikła)*, spiced up by a horseradish dressing, is a popular choice. Salad dressings tend to be based on mayonnaise, often flavoured and enriched with sour cream or chopped hard-boiled eggs.

Serves 4
450g/1lb/6½ cups fresh wild mushrooms
60ml/4 tbsp butter
2 large onions, halved and sliced
15ml/1 tbsp plain (all-purpose) flour
250ml/8fl oz/1 cup sour cream
salt and ground black pepper, to taste
15ml/1 tbsp chopped fresh parsley,
  to garnish

Sautéed Wild Mushrooms
Duszone grzyby

Poland is the largest producer of wild mushrooms in Europe, and collecting them is a common pastime. This recipe of fried onions and mushrooms in a sour cream sauce allows the earthy flavours to shine through, and can be served as an accompaniment to fried or roasted meat.

1 Brush the wild mushrooms to remove any grit and wash the caps only briefly if necessary. Dry the mushrooms with kitchen paper and slice them thinly.

2 Melt the butter in a large frying pan, then add the onions. Cook gently for 5 minutes, or until they begin to brown slightly. Stir in the flour and sour cream.

3 Add the sliced mushrooms and season to taste. Simmer gently over a low heat for 15 minutes.

4 Garnish with chopped parsley and serve immediately.

PER SERVING: Energy 303kcal/1253kJ; Protein 5.5g; Carbohydrate 13.7g, of which sugars 8.4g; Fat 25.6g, of which saturates 15.8g; Cholesterol 69mg; Calcium 98mg; Fibre 2.8g; Sodium 125mg.

Spiced Red Cabbage
Czerwona kapusta

Red cabbage is one of the staples of Polish cooking. Here, it is braised with apples and aromatic spices and makes the perfect accompaniment to goose or duck.

Serves 4–6
1 tbsp butter
1 large onion, sliced
1 red cabbage, finely shredded
2 cooking apples, peeled, cored
  and cut into cubes
7.5ml/1½ tsp caraway seeds
4–5 bay leaves
5–6 allspice berries
30ml/2 tbsp clear honey
juice of 1 lemon
1 glass dry red wine
6 whole cloves
salt and ground black pepper,
  to taste
chopped chives or parsley,
  to garnish

1 Melt the butter in a frying pan over a medium heat.

2 Add the sliced onion to the frying pan and fry gently for 5 minutes, or until the onion has softened and is golden brown.

3 Put the shredded cabbage in a large, heavy pan, and pour over 1 litre/1¾ pints/4 cups boiling water.

4 Add the onion to the cabbage with the remaining ingredients. Stir well and cover. Cook over a medium heat for 15–20 minutes.

5 Check the mixture towards the end of the cooking time. The cabbage should be tender, the apples should have broken down and the liquid should have reduced by about half.

6 If there is too much liquid, cook uncovered for a further 5 minutes.

7 Add salt and ground black pepper to taste, if you wish.

8 Serve immediately, garnished with chopped chives or parsley.

PER SERVING: Energy 112kcal/469kJ; Protein 2g; Carbohydrate 17.1g, of which sugars 15.5g; Fat 2.4g, of which saturates 1.3g; Cholesterol 5mg; Calcium 55mg; Fibre 3.1g; Sodium 25mg.

Serves 4

1kg/2¼lb potatoes, peeled
2 eggs, beaten
pinch of salt
115g/4oz plain (all-purpose) flour,
  plus extra for dusting
15ml/1 tbsp potato flour
150g/5oz pork fat *(boczek)*, cut into
  1cm/½in cubes

Grated Potato Dumplings Pyzy

These dumplings contain a mixture of mashed and grated potato, which gives them an interesting texture. They make an ideal accompaniment to many casseroled or braised meat dishes and can be served with fried cubes of pork fat.

1 Chop half the potatoes into chunks, then add to a pan of lightly salted boiling water. Cook for 10 minutes, or until soft. Drain the potatoes, then mash in a large bowl.

2 Grate the remaining raw potatoes and squeeze in a sieve to remove the excess liquid. Add to the mashed potato in the bowl.

3 Add the eggs, a pinch of salt and the flours to the bowl, and knead thoroughly to form a dough.

4 Using floured hands, roll spoonfuls of the dough into balls.

5 Bring a large pan of lightly salted water to the boil, then add the dumplings. Cook for 4–5 minutes, or until the dumplings float to the surface of the water.

6 Meanwhile, fry the cubes of pork fat in a hot pan for about 4 minutes, or until golden brown all over.

7 Transfer the cooked dumplings to a serving plate and spoon over the fried pork fat cubes.

PER SERVING: Energy 658kcal/2746kJ; Protein 10.3g; Carbohydrate 65.6g, of which sugars 3.7g; Fat 41.1g, of which saturates 16.2g; Cholesterol 130mg; Calcium 71mg; Fibre 3.5g; Sodium 64mg.

Serves 4–6
5 potatoes, unpeeled
225g/8oz/2 cups plain
    (all-purpose) flour
1 egg, beaten
2.5ml/½ tsp salt
45ml/3 tbsp butter
45ml/3 tbsp fresh white
    breadcrumbs

Mashed Potato Dumplings
Kopytka

These soft little dumplings, which are similar to Italian gnocchi, can be served with different toppings. Here they are served with a crisp breadcrumb topping, adding texture and colour to the dumplings. They make an excellent accompaniment to braised meats.

1 Cut the potatoes into quarters. Place in a pan of boiling water and cook for 10–15 minutes, or until tender. Remove from the heat, drain and leave to cool.

2 Push the potatoes through a ricer, or mash to a paste with a potato masher. Add the flour, egg and salt, and knead to combine.

3 Transfer the dough to a lightly floured surface and, with damp hands, shape into walnut-sized balls. Flatten the balls slightly and make a small indentation in the centre.

4 Bring a large pan of lightly salted water to the boil, then drop in the dumplings and cook for 5 minutes, or until they are firm to the touch.

5 Meanwhile, melt the butter in a frying pan, add the breadcrumbs and fry for about 3 minutes, or until the breadcrumbs are brown.

6 Drain the dumplings and arrange on a serving dish. Sprinkle the browned breadcrumbs over the top, and serve immediately.

PER SERVING: Energy 313kcal/1321kJ; Protein 7.5g; Carbohydrate 56g, of which sugars 2.8g; Fat 8.1g, of which saturates 4.4g; Cholesterol 48mg; Calcium 69mg; Fibre 2.8g; Sodium 240mg.

Potato and Cheese Dumplings
Pierogi

Originating from old Slavic folk cuisine, *pierogi* are popular all over Poland. Made from simple, cheap ingredients, they can be served immediately after they are cooked, or allowed to cool and then fried in a little butter. They can be filled with a number of different stuffings, including meat and onion, mushrooms and cabbage, blueberries, sweet cherries, or, as here, with potato and curd cheese.

Serves 4–6

500g/1¼ lb plain (all-purpose) flour,
  plus extra for dusting
2.5ml/½ tsp salt
2 eggs, beaten
45ml/3 tbsp vegetable oil
250ml/8fl oz/1 cup warm water
chopped fresh parsley, to garnish
thick sour cream, to serve

For the filling

15g/½oz/1 tbsp butter
½ large onion, finely chopped
250g/9oz peeled, cooked potatoes
250g/9oz/1¼ cups curd or cream cheese
1 egg, beaten
salt and ground black pepper, to taste

1 To make the filling, heat the butter in a small pan, add the onion and cook for about 5 minutes, or until softened.

2 Push the cooked potatoes through a ricer, or mash in a large bowl. Add the cheese and stir to combine thoroughly. Add the egg, onion and seasoning to taste to the potato mixture and mix well.

3 To make the dough, sift the flour into a large bowl, then add the salt and the two eggs. Pour in the oil and water, and mix to form a loose dough.

4 Turn out on to a floured surface and knead well for about 10 minutes, or until the dough is pliant and does not stick to the work surface or your hands.

5 Divide the dough into four equal pieces, then roll each one out thinly with a floured rolling pin. (Cover the portions you are not working with with a dish towel to prevent them from drying out.) Cut the dough into 5–6cm/2–2½in circles using a pastry (cookie) cutter.

6 Place a heaped teaspoonful of the cheese filling mixture in the centre of each of the circles of dough, then fold over the dough and press firmly to seal the edges. The dumplings should be neat and well filled, but not bursting.

7 Bring a large pan of lightly salted water to the boil, add the dumplings and cook for about 4–5 minutes, or until they rise to the surface.

8 Cook for a further 2 minutes, once they have risen, then remove with a slotted spoon and place in a warmed serving dish. Garnish with chopped parsley and serve with thick sour cream.

PER SERVING: Energy 419kcal/1768kJ; Protein 11.7g; Carbohydrate 71.6g, of which sugars 2.3g; Fat 11.5g, of which saturates 2.9g; Cholesterol 100mg; Calcium 136mg; Fibre 3.1g; Sodium 57mg.

Dumplings Stuffed with Mushrooms
Uszka do zupy

These tiny stuffed dumplings are traditionally served as an accompaniment to borscht or clear soup, or as a light snack with a shot of 95 per cent proof Polish spirit or vodka. *Uszka* means "little ears" in Polish, and it is generally thought that the smaller the dumplings the greater the skill of the cook who made them.

Serves 4–6

225g/8oz/2 cups plain (all-purpose) flour, plus extra for dusting
2.5ml/½ tsp salt
1 egg, beaten
30–45ml/2–3 tbsp lukewarm water
chopped fresh parsley, to garnish (optional)

For the filling

115g/4oz/2 cups dried mushrooms, rinsed and soaked in warm water for 30 minutes
25g/1oz/2 tbsp butter
1 onion, very finely chopped
15ml/1 tbsp fresh white breadcrumbs
30ml/2 tbsp finely chopped fresh parsley
1 egg, beaten
salt and ground black pepper, to taste

1 To make the filling, drain the soaked mushrooms and chop very finely. Gently heat the butter in a large frying pan, add the onion and sauté for 5 minutes, or until softened.

2 Add the chopped mushrooms to the pan and cook for about 10 minutes, or until the liquid has evaporated and the mixture begins to sizzle.

3 Turn the mushroom mixture into a large bowl, then add the fresh white breadcrumbs, chopped parsley and egg. Season to taste and mix together to form a firm paste, then set aside and leave to cool slightly. (This mixture can be kept in the refrigerator for up to 24 hours.)

4 Sift the flour into a large bowl, mix in the salt, then make a dip in the middle with the back of a wooden spoon. Put the egg in the dip and stir in enough lukewarm water to form a stiff dough.

5 Turn the dough out on to a lightly floured surface and knead until the dough is pliant but fairly stiff. Leave to rest for 30 minutes. Roll out the dough thinly, to a thickness of about 3mm/⅛in, then cut into 5cm/2in squares.

6 Place a small amount of the mushroom filling in the centre of each square of dough. Fold one corner over the filling diagonally and press the edges together. Fold the two bottom corners of the triangle to the middle and press together to form a "pig's ear" shape.

7 Bring a large pan of lightly salted water to the boil. Drop in the dumplings and cook for about 3–5 minutes, or until they float to the surface.

8 Lift out the dumplings with a slotted spoon and place on a warmed serving dish. Garnish with chopped parsley, if you like, and serve immediately.

PER SERVING: Energy 198kcal/835kJ; Protein 6.4g; Carbohydrate 32g, of which sugars 1.3g; Fat 5.9g, of which saturates 2.8g; Cholesterol 72mg; Calcium 70mg; Fibre 1.5g; Sodium 70mg.

Serves 4–6

300g/11oz/1½ cups buckwheat
500ml/17fl oz/2¼ cups water
pinch of salt
60ml/4 tbsp vegetable oil or
   45g/1½oz lard

Buckwheat Kasha
Kasza gryczana

Kasha has been eaten in Poland and other eastern European countries for centuries as a staple accompaniment to all kinds of roasts and stews, although it also tastes fabulous simply served with standard or soured milk.

1 Put the buckwheat in a large, heavy pan and add the water, salt and oil or lard.

2 Bring to the boil and cook over a low heat for about 20 minutes, or until the buckwheat has absorbed all the water and the grains are soft.

3 Serve immediately.

COOK'S TIP
Kasha can be made with other grains, but the buckwheat version has a stronger flavour than most. It forms part of the traditional Christmas Eve supper.

PER SERVING: Energy 180kcal/746kJ; Protein 2.9g; Carbohydrate 25.7g, of which sugars 0g; Fat 7.8g, of which saturates 0.9g; Cholesterol 0mg; Calcium 10mg; Fibre 0g; Sodium 0mg.

Serves 4–6
2 medium cucumbers
2.5ml/½ tsp salt
120ml/4fl oz/½ cup sour cream
juice from ½ lemon
2.5ml/½ tsp sugar (optional)
1.5ml/¼ tsp ground black pepper
15ml/1 tbsp chopped fresh dill or chives,
   to garnish

Polish-style Cucumber Salad
Mizeria

According to legend, this simple salad was a favourite dish of Queen Bona Sforza, an Italian princess who married the Polish king Sigismund I in the 16th century. Homesick for her native Italy, the dish made her cry, hence its Polish name, derived from the Latin for "misery".

1 Peel the cucumbers, slice them thinly and place in a sieve (strainer).

2 Sprinkle over the salt, leave for a few minutes, then rinse to remove the salt and pat dry with kitchen paper.

3 To make the dressing, mix together the sour cream, lemon juice, sugar, if using, and black pepper.

4 Fold in the cucumber, then place in the refrigerator and leave for 1 hour.

5 Serve as an accompaniment, garnished with chopped dill or chives.

PER SERVING: Energy 48kcal/196kJ; Protein 1.1g; Carbohydrate 1.8g, of which sugars 1.7g; Fat 4.1g, of which saturates 2.5g; Cholesterol 12mg; Calcium 31mg; Fibre 0.4g; Sodium 10mg.

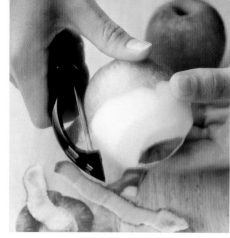

Serves 4

2 slim leeks, white part only,
  washed thoroughly
2 large apples
15ml/1 tbsp chopped fresh parsley
juice of 1 lemon
15ml/1 tbsp clear honey
salt and ground black pepper,
  to taste

Apple and Leek Salad
Sałatka z jabłek i porów

Fresh and tangy, this simple salad of sliced leeks and apples with a lemon and honey dressing can be served with a range of cold meats as part of a summer meal. For the best result, make sure you use slim young leeks and tart, crisp apples.

1 Thinly slice the leeks. Peel and core the apples, then slice thinly.

2 Put in a large serving bowl and add the parsley, lemon juice, honey and seasoning to taste.

3 Toss well, then leave to stand in a cool place for about an hour, to allow the flavours to blend together.

COOK'S TIP
When buying leeks, look for slim ones with firm white stems and bright green leaves. Avoid those that are discoloured in any way.

PER SERVING: Energy 59kcal/252kJ; Protein 1.9g; Carbohydrate 12.5g, of which sugars 11.8g; Fat 0.6g, of which saturates 0.1g; Cholesterol 0mg; Calcium 27mg; Fibre 3.4g; Sodium 4mg.

Serves 4–6
4–5 medium-sized raw beetroots (beets)
15ml/1 tbsp sugar
60–75ml/4–5 tbsp freshly grated
   horseradish
juice of 1 lemon
1 glass dry red wine
2.5ml/½ tsp salt
cold meats, to serve

Beetroot Salad
Ćwikła

The fresh, sweet and nutty flavour of beetroot makes the ideal partner for horseradish, and this salad is often served as a side dish with cold meats, such as ham and Polish sausage. Beetroot is believed to have beauty-enhancing and aphrodisiac properties.

1 Put the beetroots, in their skins, in a large pan, and pour over enough water to cover.

2 Bring to the boil and cook the beetroots for about 1 hour, or until the beetroots are tender. Remove from the heat and leave to cool.

3 Peel and shred the beetroots finely. Put the shredded beetroots in a large jar with the sugar, horseradish, lemon juice, red wine and salt.

4 Cover tightly and store in a cool place for up to 4 months. Serve the beetroots with a range of cold meats.

PER SERVING: Energy 60kcal/253kJ; Protein 1.5g; Carbohydrate 9g, of which sugars 8.5g; Fat 0.1g, of which saturates 0g; Cholesterol 0mg; Calcium 20mg; Fibre 1.6g; Sodium 221mg.

DESSERTS

Apricot Purée with Almonds

Pear and Raspberry Compote

Wild Strawberries with
Whipped Cream

Chocolate and Coffee Mousse

Baked Coffee Custards

Polish Cheesecake

Pancakes with Vanilla Cheese

Poached Pears with
Chocolate

Plum Dumplings

Fresh and Fruity

Despite the hearty nature of many Polish main courses, diners usually find room for a dessert. Many of these are based on fruit, so they round the meal off with a sweet taste but are generally not too filling. Apricot Purée with Almonds *(Morelowy deser)* is just such a dish, made with a blend of dried apricots and almonds, with or without the alcoholic kick of vodka.

More substantial desserts, such as pancakes or cheesecake, are often based on curd cheese and eggs. Polish Cheesecake *(Sernik)* is a light baked mixture made with whisked egg whites and enriched with the yolks. Unlike cheesecakes from other countries it is not made on a biscuit or pastry base. Pancakes with Vanilla Cheese *(Naleśniki ze serem)* are folded round a similar mixture of curd cheese with raisins and vanilla, and Baked Coffee Custards *(Kawowy budyń)* make an individual sweet treat.

Serves 6
350g/12oz/½ cup dried apricots,
  finely chopped
60ml/4 tbsp water
50g/2oz/¼ cup caster (superfine) sugar
90ml/6 tbsp 95 per cent proof Polish spirit
75g/3oz/½ cup blanched almonds, chopped
75g/3oz/½ cup chopped candied peel
whipped cream and ground cinnamon,
  to serve

Apricot Purée with Almonds
Morelowy deser

Many traditional Polish desserts are made with dried fruits, such as plums, apricots or apples, because it was once difficult to buy the fresh variety out of season. This rich apricot purée is warming and nutritious, making it especially popular during the winter.

1 Place the chopped apricots and the water in a heavy pan, bring to the boil and simmer for 25 minutes.

2 Add the sugar and simmer for a further 10 minutes, or until you have a thick jam-like mixture.

3 Remove from the heat and stir in the Polish spirit, almonds and candied peel.

4 Spoon into serving dishes or glasses and leave to cool, then chill in the refrigerator for at least 2 hours. Just before serving, decorate with whipped cream and dust with cinnamon.

PER SERVING: Energy 230kcal/973kJ; Protein 5.1g; Carbohydrate 38.3g, of which sugars 37.9g; Fat 7.4g, of which saturates 0.6g; Cholesterol 0mg; Calcium 93mg; Fibre 5.2g; Sodium 46mg.

Serves 4–6
900ml/1½ pint/3¾ cups water
350g/12oz/1¾ cups sugar
1 large cinnamon stick
4–5 whole cloves
900g/2lb pears, peeled, cored and
    cut into quarters
275g/10oz/1⅔ cups fresh
    raspberries, rinsed
60ml/4 tbsp raspberry liqueur

Pear and Raspberry Compote
Gruszkowy malinowy kompot

This simple dessert combines seasonal fruit with typical Polish flavourings, cinnamon and cloves, to make a nutritious dish that can be eaten on its own or served with vanilla ice cream or whipped cream. Omit the raspberry liqueur if you are making this for children.

1 Place the water and sugar in a heavy pan and heat gently until the sugar has dissolved.

2 Add the cinnamon stick and cloves to the mixture, increase the heat and boil for 4 minutes, stirring, until the mixture becomes syrupy.

3 Add the pears to the pan and simmer gently over a low heat for 15–20 minutes, or until the pears are tender. Lift out the pears with a slotted spoon and arrange on a serving dish. Leave to cool.

4 Meanwhile, remove the cinnamon and cloves from the syrup in the pan.

5 Blend half the raspberries in a food processor, then push through a sieve set over a bowl and add the juices to the syrup in the pan. Stir in the remaining raspberries and the raspberry liqueur.

6 Pour the sauce over the pears and leave to cool completely before chilling in the refrigerator. Alternatively, serve the compote warm.

PER SERVING: Energy 331kcal/1408kJ; Protein 1.6g; Carbohydrate 81.9g, of which sugars 81.9g; Fat 0.3g, of which saturates 0.1g; Cholesterol 0mg; Calcium 63mg; Fibre 4.8g; Sodium 11mg.

Serves 4
475ml/16fl oz/2 cups double
  (heavy) cream
50g/2oz/¼ cup vanilla sugar
275g/10oz/2½ cups wild strawberries
fresh mint leaves, to decorate

Wild Strawberries with Whipped Cream
Poziomki z bitą śmietaną

Smaller and with a more intense flavour than their domestic cousins, wild strawberries require little in the way of preparation. In this delectable dish they are simply served with a dollop of slightly sweetened cream and garnished with mint.

1 Whip the double cream with the sugar until soft peaks form.

2 Wash and hull the berries, then divide among four serving dishes.

3 Spoon over the sweetened whipped cream and decorate with fresh mint. Serve immediately.

COOK'S TIP
Tiny wild strawberries grow on grassy banks, heaths and open woodland and have a beautifully sweet flavour. The plant, which has hairy stems and runners, is low-growing and the leaves are toothed, shiny and grow in groups of three. Look for the ripe berries in mid- to late summer.

PER SERVING: Energy 657kcal/2712kJ; Protein 2.5g; Carbohydrate 19.2g, of which sugars 19.2g; Fat 63.8g, of which saturates 39.7g; Cholesterol 163mg; Calcium 76mg; Fibre 0.8g; Sodium 31mg.

Serves 4–6
250g/9oz dark (bittersweet) chocolate
   (minimum 70 per cent cocoa solids)
60ml/4 tbsp cooled strong black coffee
8 eggs, separated
200g/7oz/1 cup caster
   (superfine) sugar
60ml/4 tbsp rum, or 95 per cent
   proof Polish spirit or vodka

Chocolate and Coffee Mousse
Mus czekoladowy

A light chocolate mousse is always a popular way to end a meal. This Polish version is made with a good strong chocolate flavoured with coffee and rum, Polish spirit or vodka. You can omit all or any of these, depending on your preference.

1 Break the chocolate into small pieces and melt in a heatproof bowl over a pan of gently simmering water. Ensure the water does not touch the base of the bowl, or the chocolate may seize.

2 Once the chocolate has completely melted, stir in the cold coffee. Leave to cool slightly.

3 Beat the egg yolks with half the sugar until it is pale, thick and creamy. Add the rum, Polish spirit or vodka and stir in the melted chocolate mixture.

4 Whisk the egg whites in a separate bowl until stiff peaks form.

5 Stir in the remaining sugar, then fold into the chocolate mixture. Spoon into chilled glasses or ramekins. Chill for at least an hour before serving.

VARIATION
For a slightly less intense mousse, whip 300ml/½ pint/1¼ cups double (heavy) cream until soft peaks form, then fold in to the mixture at the end of step 3.

PER SERVING: Energy 464kcal/1951kJ; Protein 10.6g; Carbohydrate 61.3g, of which sugars 60.9g; Fat 19.1g, of which saturates 9.1g; Cholesterol 256mg; Calcium 70mg; Fibre 1.1g; Sodium 98mg.

Serves 4

300ml/½ pint/1¼ cups full-fat
  (whole) milk
25g/1oz ground coffee (not instant)
150ml/¼ pint/⅔ cup single (light) cream
3 eggs
30ml/2 tbsp caster (superfine) sugar
whipped cream and cocoa powder,
  to serve

Baked Coffee Custards
Kawowy budyń

Unlike their eastern European neighbours, the Polish have a passion for both drinking and cooking with coffee. Here, it is used to lift a simple baked custard to new heights.

1 Preheat the oven to 190°C/375°F/ Gas 5. Put the milk in a heavy pan and bring to the boil. Add the coffee, remove from the heat and leave to infuse for 10 minutes.

2 Strain the flavoured milk into a clean pan, add the cream and gently heat until just simmering.

3 Beat the eggs and sugar in a bowl until pale and fluffy. Pour over the hot milk mixture, whisking constantly.

4 Pour the custard mixture into individual heatproof bowls or coffee cups and cover tightly with foil. Place them in a roasting pan and pour in enough boiling water to come halfway up the bowls or cups.

5 Carefully place the roasting pan in the oven and cook for about 30 minutes, or until the custards are set. Remove from the roasting pan and leave to cool completely. Transfer to the refrigerator and chill for at least 2 hours.

6 Just before serving, decorate the top with whipped cream and dust with cocoa powder.

PER SERVING: Energy 207kcal/860kJ; Protein 8.5g; Carbohydrate 12g, of which sugars 12g; Fat 14.3g, of which saturates 7.6g; Cholesterol 174mg; Calcium 147mg; Fibre 0g; Sodium 96mg.

Serves 6–8

500g/1¼ lb/2¼ cups curd (farmer's) cheese
100g/3¾oz/scant ½ cup butter, softened
2.5ml/½ tsp vanilla extract
6 eggs, separated
150g/5oz/¾ cup caster (superfine) sugar
10ml/2 tsp grated lemon rind
15ml/1 tbsp cornflour (cornstarch)
15ml/1 tbsp semolina
50g/5oz/⅓ cup raisins or sultanas
  (golden raisins) (optional)
icing (confectioners') sugar, to dust

Polish Cheesecake
Sernik

There are many versions of *sernik* in Poland, including this light version that is not made on a biscuit base.

COOK'S TIP
It is important to use good quality curd cheese in this recipe; it should not taste sour at all.

1 Preheat the oven to 200°C/400°F/ Gas 6. Grease and line a 20cm/8in round cake tin (pan).

2 Cream together the curd cheese, butter and vanilla in a large bowl until combined.

3 In a separate large bowl, whisk the egg whites with 15ml/1 tbsp sugar, until stiff peaks form.

4 In a third bowl, whisk the egg yolks with the remaining sugar until the mixture is thick and creamy.

5 Add the egg yolk and sugar mixture to the curd cheese and butter mixture with the lemon rind and stir to combine.

6 Gently fold in the egg whites, then the cornflour, semolina and raisins or sultanas, if using, taking care not to knock the air out of the mixture.

7 Transfer the mixture to the prepared tin and bake for 1 hour, or until set and golden brown.

8 Leave to cool in the tin, then dust with icing sugar and serve in slices.

PER SERVING: Energy 347kcal/1448kJ; Protein 10.8g; Carbohydrate 24.8g, of which sugars 21.6g; Fat 23.6g, of which saturates 13.4g; Cholesterol 196mg; Calcium 34mg; Fibre 0g; Sodium 131mg.

Serves 4–6

115g/4oz/1 cup plain (all-purpose) flour
45ml/3 tbsp sugar
pinch of salt
3 eggs, plus 2 yolks
350ml/12fl oz/1½ cups milk
225g/8oz/1 cup curd (farmer's) cheese
40g/1½oz/¼ cup raisins
45ml/3 tbsp rum
10ml/2 tsp vanilla sugar or 5ml/1 tsp
   vanilla extract
45ml/3 tbsp vegetable oil
45ml/3 tbsp icing (confectioners') sugar,
   for dusting

VARIATION
These pancakes are delicious served with Sautéed Wild Mushrooms (see page 86). Simply omit the sugar from the batter mix.

Pancakes with Vanilla Cheese
Naleśniki ze serem

Pancakes are always popular, and these delicious Polish ones are no exception. Filled with a rich rum and raisin cheese mixture, the pancakes are dusted with icing sugar.

1 Sift the flour into a large bowl. Stir in the sugar and salt, and make a well in the centre.

2 Whisk together the 3 eggs and the milk. Gradually add the milk mixture to the flour, beating constantly, until you have a smooth batter.

3 Put the egg yolks, curd cheese, raisins, rum and vanilla sugar or extract in a bowl and beat well.

4 Heat enough oil to just coat the base of a small frying pan over a high heat and add a ladleful of the pancake batter.

5 Cook for about 1 minute, until golden underneath, then flip over and cook on the other side. Slide on to a plate and keep warm. Continue until you have used all the batter.

6 Place a spoonful of the curd cheese mixture in the centre of each pancake and fold the edges over to completely enclose the filling.

7 Dust the pancakes with icing sugar and serve immediately.

PER SERVING: Energy 330kcal/1383kJ; Protein 11.5g; Carbohydrate 31.3g, of which sugars 16.7g; Fat 16.8g, of which saturates 6g; Cholesterol 182mg; Calcium 126mg; Fibre 0.7g; Sodium 68mg.

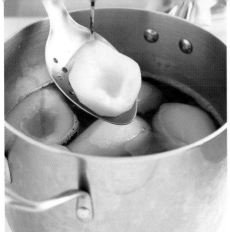

Serves 4

4 firm dessert pears, peeled
250g/9oz/1¼ cups caster (superfine) sugar
600ml/1 pint/2½ cups water
500ml/17fl oz/2¼ cups vanilla ice cream

For the chocolate sauce

250g/9oz good quality dark (bittersweet)
  chocolate (minimum 70 per cent
  cocoa solids)
40g/1½oz unsalted (sweet) butter
5ml/1 tsp vanilla extract
75ml/5 tbsp double (heavy) cream

Poached Pears with Chocolate
Gruszki w czekoladzie

Many types of pear are grown in Poland, and they are
either simply eaten raw or gently poached and served
with a rich chocolate sauce, as in this recipe.

VARIATION
Like apples, there are two types of pear:
dessert varieties and those that require
cooking. Try to ensure that you use firm
ones, as they will hold their shape when
poached, rather than disintegrating.

1 Cut the pears in half lengthways
and remove the core. Place the
sugar and water in a large pan and
gently heat until the sugar has
dissolved completely.

2 Add the pear halves to the pan,
then simmer for about 20 minutes,
or until the pears are tender but not
falling apart. Lift out of the sugar
syrup with a slotted spoon and leave
to cool.

3 To make the chocolate sauce, break
the chocolate into small pieces and
put into a pan.

4 Add the butter and 30ml/2 tbsp
water. Heat gently over a low heat,
without stirring, until the chocolate
has melted.

5 Add the vanilla extract and cream,
and mix gently to combine.

6 Place a scoop of ice cream into
each of four glasses.

7 Add two cooled pear halves to each
and pour over the hot chocolate
sauce. Serve immediately.

PER SERVING: Energy 1014kcal/4255kJ; Protein 8.8g; Carbohydrate 145.1g, of which sugars 143.2g; Fat 46.7g, of which saturates 29.6g; Cholesterol 81mg; Calcium 206mg; Fibre 4.9g; Sodium 152mg.

Plum Dumplings
Knedle ze śliwkami

These traditional sweet dumplings, made with a potato dough, contain a whole plum, stuffed with cinnamon sugar. They are served everywhere in Poland during the autumn, when plums are at their best – sometimes as a meal on their own!

Serves 4–6

675g/1½lb potatoes, peeled
250ml/8fl oz/1 cup sour cream
75g/3oz/6 tbsp butter
2 eggs, beaten
250g/9oz/2¼ cups plain (all-purpose) flour, plus extra for dusting
8–12 plums
90g/3½oz/¾ cup icing (confectioners') sugar
30ml/2 tbsp ground cinnamon
45ml/3 tbsp breadcrumbs
icing (confectioners') sugar and cinnamon, for dusting

1 Cut the potatoes into even-sized pieces and cook in a pan of lightly salted boiling water for 10–15 minutes, or until soft. Drain, leave to cool, then mash in a large bowl.

2 Add the sour cream, 25g/1oz/2 tbsp butter, eggs and flour to the mashed potato and stir to combine thoroughly.

3 Turn the dough out on to a lightly floured surface and knead lightly until the dough comes together and is firm. Add a little more flour if necessary – it should not be sticky.

4 Cut a slit down one side of each plum so that you can remove the stone (pit) while keeping the plum intact. Mix together the icing sugar and cinnamon, then push a teaspoonful into each of the plums.

5 Roll out the dough to 5mm/¼in thick and cut into eight or twelve 10cm/4in squares (depending on how many plums you have). Place a plum in the centre of each square, then bring up the dough and pinch the edges together to completely seal the plum in the dough.

6 Bring a large pan of water to the boil, and add the dumplings in batches of about six at a time. Cook for about 8 minutes, or until they rise to the surface. Remove with a slotted spoon, transfer to a bowl and keep warm while you cook the remaining dumplings.

7 Heat the remaining butter in a large frying pan, add the breadcrumbs and fry for a few minutes, until golden brown. Add the dumplings and gently turn in the breadcrumbs to coat.

8 Transfer to a warm serving plate and dust with icing sugar and cinnamon. Serve immediately.

PER SERVING: Energy 510kcal/2147kJ; Protein 11.1g; Carbohydrate 72.6g, of which sugars 18.6g; Fat 21.6g, of which saturates 12.4g; Cholesterol 115mg; Calcium 147mg; Fibre 5.3g; Sodium 190mg.

BAKING

Sweet and sumptuous

The Poles undeniably have a sweet tooth, and this is amply satisfied by their many recipes for delectable treats. Although people do make cakes and cookies at home, bakeries take pride in creating beautifully decorated cakes and pastries to eat as a dessert or snack.

The best cakes and pastries are traditionally made at Christmas and Easter, although they are often eaten at other times of the year too. The tall, fluted shape of the Easter Cake *(Babka wielkanocna)* makes a great centrepiece for the dining table on Easter Sunday, as does Poppy Seed Cake *(Makowiec)*, a favourite at both Easter and Christmas.

Many cake recipes are made with a yeast dough rather than using other raising agents such as baking powder. This gives a firm texture and a distinctive flavour that is ideal for combining with dried fruit and spices.

Makes 20

225g/8oz/1 cup clear honey
4 eggs, plus 2 egg whites
350g/12oz/3 cups plain
  (all-purpose) flour
5ml/1 tsp bicarbonate of soda
  (baking soda)
2.5ml/½ tsp freshly grated nutmeg
2.5ml/½ tsp ground ginger
2.5ml/½ tsp ground cinnamon
2.5ml/½ tsp ground cloves
20 blanched almond halves

COOK'S TIPS

Ancient Slavic tribes used to make cakes with honey, but it wasn't until the arrival of spices like ginger, cinnamon and cloves in the 17th century that Polish people starting making these sweet and delicious little morsels.

Honey and Almond Cookies
Pierniki z migdałami

These delectable spiced honey cookies are traditionally made at Christmas, although they are also eaten at other times of the year.

1 Beat together the honey and whole eggs until light and fluffy. Sift over the flour, bicarbonate of soda and spices, and beat to combine.

2 Gather the cookie dough into a ball, wrap in clear film (plastic wrap) and chill in the refrigerator for 1 hour or overnight.

3 Preheat the oven to 200°C/400°F/ Gas 6. Roll out the dough on a lightly floured surface to a thickness of 5mm/¼in. Using a 4cm/1½in cookie cutter, stamp out 20 rounds.

4 Transfer the rounds to two lightly greased baking trays. Beat the egg whites until soft peaks form. Brush the tops of the rounds with the egg white, then press an almond half into the centre of each one.

5 Place in the oven and bake for 15–20 minutes, or until they are a pale golden brown.

6 Remove from the oven and allow to cool slightly before transferring to a wire cooling rack. Leave to cool completely, then serve.

PER COOKIE: Energy 112kcal/473kJ; Protein 3.4g; Carbohydrate 22.6g, of which sugars 8.9g; Fat 1.5g, of which saturates 0.4g; Cholesterol 38mg; Calcium 33mg; Fibre 0.5g; Sodium 22mg.

Serves 4–6

50g/2oz/¼ cup butter, softened
50g/2oz/¼ cup caster (superfine) sugar
3 egg yolks, plus 1 whole egg
250g/9oz/2¼ cups plain (all-purpose)
    flour, plus extra for dusting
2.5ml/½ tsp bicarbonate of soda
    (baking soda)
120ml/4fl oz/½ cup sour cream
pinch of salt
30ml/2 tbsp clear honey
45ml/3 tbsp 95 per cent proof Polish
    spirit or vodka, or rum
15ml/1 tbsp vinegar
vegetable oil, for deep-frying
icing (confectioner's) sugar,
    for dusting

Angel's Wings Chrusty

This Old Polish recipe for deep-fried pastry strips dusted with sugar is traditionally made on Fat Thursday, the last Thursday before Lent, and at carnivals.

COOK'S TIPS

• Add a cube of bread to the hot oil to prevent it from spitting while the cookies are cooking.
• These cookies are delicious eaten warm or cold, but for the best flavour and texture they should be eaten on the day they are made.

1 Beat the butter and sugar in a large bowl.

2 Add the eggs, flour, bicarbonate of soda, sour cream, salt, honey, Polish spirit, vodka or rum, and the vinegar.

3 Beat to combine thoroughly and to form a smooth dough.

4 Transfer the dough to a lightly floured surface and roll out a long, thin rectangle, 10cm/4in across, to a thickness of 3mm/⅛in.

5 Cut the dough lengthways into four 2.5cm/1in strips, then cut each of these horizontally, on a slight slant, into pieces about 10cm/4in long.

6 Make a 4cm/1½in lengthways slit in the middle of each strip.

7 Lift the lower end of the pastry and pass it through the slit.

8 Gently pull it through the other side and downwards to create a twist in the pastry.

9 Heat enough oil for deep-frying to 180°C/350°F/Gas 4, then add the pastry strips in batches of two and fry for 5–8 seconds, until they rise to the surface and are golden brown.

10 Remove from the oil immediately, using a slotted spoon, and drain on kitchen paper.

11 Repeat the process with the remaining pastry.

12 Transfer to a serving dish and dust generously with icing sugar.

PER SERVING: Energy 364kcal/1527kJ; Protein 7.7g; Carbohydrate 45.7g, of which sugars 14g; Fat 16.2g, of which saturates 8.3g; Cholesterol 203mg; Calcium 104mg; Fibre 1.3g; Sodium 79mg.

Easter Pastry
Mazurek

Consumed in vast quantities at Easter, there are many different toppings for these sweet, decorative pastries, including nut paste, almonds, cheese, jams, raisins and coloured icing. This version is made with a rich vanilla cream and studded with almonds and dried fruit.

Serves 6

300g/11oz/2⅔ cups plain
  (all-purpose) flour
115g/4oz/1 cup icing
  (confectioners') sugar
250g/9oz/generous 1 cup butter,
  softened
4 egg yolks

For the filling

500ml/17fl oz/2¼ cups double
  (heavy) cream
400g/14oz/2 cups caster
  (superfine) sugar
1 vanilla pod (bean)
400g/14oz/1¾ cups unsalted
  (sweet) butter
about 150g/5oz each of almonds and
  dried fruits, to decorate

COOK'S TIP
The pastry will keep for up to 3 days in an airtight container in the refrigerator.

VARIATION
You can decorate the top with anything you like. Good choices might include crystallized (candied) fruits, drizzles of chocolate, sweets (candies) or coloured icing (frosting). Children, in particular, will enjoy decorating the top.

1 Sift the flour and icing sugar into a large bowl. Add the softened butter and egg yolks, and mix thoroughly to make a smooth dough.

2 Form the dough into a ball, cover with clear film (plastic wrap) and chill in the refrigerator for 45 minutes.

3 Preheat the oven to 220°C/425°F/Gas 7. Grease a rectangular baking tray. Roll out the pastry and cut a piece that is the same size as the tray. Place on the tray.

4 Cut the remaining pastry into strips about 1cm/½in wide and join together to make one long strip. Lightly brush a little water around the edge of the pastry rectangle. Twist the strip of pastry and place over the moistened edge.

5 Bake the pastry in the oven for about 20 minutes, or until golden brown. Leave to cool slightly, then carefully lift it out on to a large serving dish and cool completely.

6 To make the filling, pour the cream into a heavy pan, then add the sugar and vanilla pod. Gently bring to the boil, then boil for about 5 minutes, stirring constantly, until the mixture is thick.

7 To test whether it is ready, spoon a small amount on to a cold plate. It should set quickly. Remove from the heat and leave to cool slightly.

8 Remove the vanilla pod, then beat in the butter while the cream mixture is still warm. Spread the mixture inside the pastry case, smoothing the top.

9 While the filling is still warm, decorate the top with almonds and dried fruits. You can either simply sprinkle the nuts and fruit over, or you may like to create a pattern.

PER SERVING: Energy 1989kcal/8270kJ; Protein 14.9g; Carbohydrate 149.4g, of which sugars 110.6g; Fat 152.2g, of which saturates 86.5g; Cholesterol 480mg; Calcium 270mg; Fibre 4g; Sodium 703mg.

Poppy Seed Cake
Makowiec

This dark, dense cake, made from a sweet dough rolled with an aromatic poppy-seed filling, is made throughout the year, but especially at Christmas and Easter.

Serves 6

45ml/3 tbsp sour cream
50g/2oz fresh yeast or 2 packets active
  dried yeast
400g/14oz/3½ cups strong white bread flour
115g/4oz/1 cup icing (confectioners') sugar
15ml/1 tbsp grated lemon rind
pinch of salt
150g/5oz/10 tbsp butter, melted and cooled
3 eggs, beaten

For the filling

500g/1¼lb/5 cups poppy seeds
200g/7oz/scant 1 cup butter
200g/7oz/1 cup sugar
115g/4oz/1 cup chopped almonds
30ml/2 tbsp currants
60ml/4 tbsp honey
45ml/3 tbsp finely chopped candied peel
1 vanilla pod (bean)
3 egg whites, lightly beaten
15ml/1 tbsp rum or cognac

1 To make the filling, place the poppy seeds in a fine mesh sieve and rinse thoroughly under cold running water. Boil a kettle and carefully pour boiling water over the seeds. Drain, then transfer to a bowl. Pour over enough boiling water to cover, then leave to soak for at least 3 hours.

2 Drain the poppy seeds, then grind as finely as possible with a pestle and mortar or in a blender.

3 Melt the butter in a pan, then add the sugar, almonds, currants, honey and candied peel. Scrape the seeds from the vanilla pod into the mixture with the poppy seeds, stir to combine, then fry gently for 20 minutes.

4 Remove from the heat, leave to cool, then stir in the beaten egg whites and rum or cognac.

5 To make the dough, mix the cream with the yeast in a small bowl. Sift the flour into a large bowl, then stir in the icing sugar, lemon rind and salt.

6 Make a well in the middle of the dry ingredients, then pour in the cooled melted butter, beaten eggs and the yeast mixture. Mix to combine, then turn out on to a lightly floured surface and knead for about 10 minutes, or until smooth and elastic.

7 Roll out the dough to a thickness of about 5mm/¼in, then spread evenly with the poppy-seed mixture. Roll up the dough to form a loaf shape and place on a greased baking tray. Cover with a clean, damp dish towel and put in a warm place to rise for 45 minutes.

8 About 10 minutes before the end of the rising time, preheat the oven to 190°C/375°F/Gas 5. Pierce the top of the loaf with a large sharp knife, then put in the hot oven and bake for 45–50 minutes, or until golden brown. Leave to cool, then slice and serve.

PER SERVING: Energy 1302kcal/5437kJ; Protein 21.9g; Carbohydrate 124.4g, of which sugars 72.9g; Fat 83.2g, of which saturates 35.9g; Cholesterol 224mg; Calcium 438mg; Fibre 6.6g; Sodium 459mg.

Serves 6–8

8 eggs, separated
125g/5oz/⅔ cup caster (superfine) sugar
165g/5½oz/scant 1½ cups walnuts,
    finely chopped
15g/1 tbsp self-raising (self-rising)
    flour, sifted

For the filling
75g/3oz/⅔ cup icing (confectioners') sugar,
    plus extra for dusting (optional)
165g/5½oz/scant 1½ cups walnuts,
    finely chopped
300ml/½ pint/1¼ cups double
    (heavy) cream
175ml/6fl oz/¾ cup 95 per cent
    proof Polish spirit or vodka,
    or cognac
½ vanilla pod (bean)
30ml/2 tbsp cold strong coffee

Walnut Gateau
Tort orzechowy

This moist walnut cake is sandwiched together with
a delectable cream, which is flavoured with coffee,
vanilla and a dash of Polish spirit, vodka or cognac.

1 Preheat the oven to 190°C/375°F/
Gas 5. Grease and line a 20cm/8in
cake tin (pan). Beat the egg yolks
with the sugar until thick and creamy.
Stir in the nuts, then fold in the flour.

2 In a separate bowl, beat the egg
whites until soft peaks form. Fold a
tablespoonful of the egg white into
the egg yolk mixture to loosen it, then
fold in the remaining egg whites. Pour
into the tin and bake for 40–45 minutes,
or until risen and brown. Allow to cool,
then turn out on to a wire rack.

3 To make the filling, combine the
icing sugar and chopped walnuts.
Whip the cream until soft peaks form,
then fold in the Polish spirit, vodka or
cognac with the walnuts and sugar.
Split the vanilla pod lengthways, then
scrape the seeds into the cream. Add
the coffee and stir to combine.

4 Split the cake into two layers. Spread
one half with two-thirds of the filling,
then position the other layer on top.

5 Spread the remaining cream on top,
dust with icing sugar, if using, and
serve cut into slices.

PER SERVING: Energy 697kcal/2889kJ; Protein 13.2g; Carbohydrate 29.5g, of which sugars 27.9g; Fat 54g, of which saturates 16.4g; Cholesterol 242mg; Calcium 106mg; Fibre 1.5g; Sodium 89mg.

Serves 4–6

15ml/1 tbsp dried yeast
120ml/4fl oz/½ cup sour cream, slightly warmed
225g/8oz/2 cups strong white bread flour, plus extra for dusting
75g/3oz/⅓ cup sugar
3 eggs, lightly beaten
15ml/1 tbsp vanilla extract
2.5ml/½ tsp almond extract
15ml/1 tbsp grated lemon rind
15ml/1 tbsp grated orange rind
40g/1½oz/¼ cup raisins

For the icing
50g/2oz/½ cup icing (confectioners') sugar
about 15ml/1 tbsp rum or lemon juice

Easter Cake
Babka wielkanocna

Served everywhere on Easter Sunday, this bread-like cake is baked in a bundt tin that is said to resemble an old woman's skirts. This gives it the name *babka*, Polish for grandmother. Finished with a rum or lemon and sugar glaze, it is as pretty as it is delicious.

1 In a bowl, combine the yeast with the sour cream. Sift half the flour into a large bowl, then stir in the sugar.

2 Add the yeast mixture, mix, then cover the bowl with a clean, damp dish towel and leave in a warm place for 1 hour, or until doubled in size.

3 Add the remaining flour with the remaining ingredients. Mix to combine, then transfer to a lightly floured surface and knead for 10 minutes, or until smooth and elastic.

4 Grease and flour a 23cm/9in bundt tin (pan). Place the dough in the mould, cover with a damp dish towel and leave in a warm place for 1 hour, or until doubled in size.

5 Meanwhile, heat the oven to 200°C/400°F/Gas 6. Put the cake in the oven and bake for 1 hour, or until the top is golden brown.

6 Leave to cool slightly in the tin, then turn out on to a wire rack and cool completely.

7 Sift the icing sugar into a large bowl and add the rum or lemon juice. Stir to make a smooth icing with a pouring consistency.

8 Place a plate underneath the cake on the wire rack and drizzle the icing over the cake.

9 Leave the icing to set, then slice the cake and serve.

PER SERVING: Energy 299kcal/1262kJ; Protein 7.5g; Carbohydrate 54.4g, of which sugars 25.8g; Fat 7.3g, of which saturates 3.4g; Cholesterol 107mg; Calcium 99mg; Fibre 1.3g; Sodium 50mg.

Chocolate and Almond Cake
Tort czekoladowy

This rich, dense chocolate cake is filled with a sweet almond paste and coated in glossy dark chocolate icing. It is often served as a snack with coffee or as an indulgent dessert for a special occasion. Store in an airtight container in the refrigerator.

Serves 6
6 eggs, separated
115g/4oz/1 cup caster (superfine) sugar
150g/5oz/1¼ cups unsweetened cocoa powder
150g/5oz/1¼ cups ground almonds

For the almond paste
150g/5oz/1¼ cups caster (superfine) sugar
120ml/4fl oz/½ cup water
150g/5oz/1¼ cups ground almonds
15–30ml/1–2 tbsp lemon juice, to taste
½ vanilla pod (bean)

For the icing
115g/4oz good quality dark (bittersweet) chocolate (minimum 70 per cent cocoa solids), chopped
25g/1oz/2 tbsp unsalted (sweet) butter, cubed
120ml/4fl oz/½ cup double (heavy) cream
50g/2oz/½ cup icing (confectioners') sugar, sifted

1 Preheat the oven to 200°C/400°F/Gas 6. Grease and line a 20cm/8in springform cake tin (pan).

2 Place the egg yolks in a large bowl and add the sugar. Beat together until the mixture is thick and creamy, then add the cocoa powder and ground almonds, and gently fold together.

3 Whisk the egg whites until stiff peaks form. Using a metal spoon, gently fold a tablespoonful of the egg white into the egg yolk mixture to loosen it slightly, then fold in the remaining egg whites.

4 Spoon the mixture into the tin and bake for 1 hour, or until a skewer inserted into the centre comes out clean. Leave to cool completely in the tin.

5 To make the almond paste, put the sugar and water in a heavy pan, then heat gently until the sugar has completely dissolved. Bring to the boil and boil for 4–6 minutes, or until a thick syrup forms. Stir in the ground almonds and bring back to the boil.

6 Transfer the paste to a bowl, then add the lemon juice. Split the vanilla pod in half and scrape the seeds into the bowl. Mix well to combine.

7 Remove the cake from the tin and carefully slice into two even layers. Spread the bottom half with the almond paste, then sandwich the second half on top.

8 To make the icing, melt the chocolate and butter in a heatproof bowl over a pan of gently simmering water, ensuring the water does not touch the bowl.

9 Remove from the heat and gently stir in the cream, then add the sifted icing sugar and stir to combine. Cover the top of the cake with the chocolate icing. Leave to set, then serve cut into slices.

PER SERVING: Energy 892kcal/3726kJ; Protein 23g; Carbohydrate 73.7g, of which sugars 69.3g; Fat 58.4g, of which saturates 19g; Cholesterol 228mg; Calcium 226mg; Fibre 7.2g; Sodium 349mg.

Index

Picture Credits:
All photography by Jon Whitaker, apart from
the following:
t = top; b = bottom; r = right; l = left
Alamy: 7tl (lookGaleria/Alamy), 11tr
(Pegaz/Alamy), 12b (lookGaleria/Alamy),
12tr (Dagmar Schwelle/Alamy), 14bl (Bon
Appetit/Alamy), 16b (lookGaleria/Alamy),
16tr (Bon Appetit/Alamy); Corbis: 7tr
(Dariusz Delmanowicz/PAP/Corbis), 9tr
(Raymon Gehman/Corbis), 10br (Lech
Muszyński/PAP/Corbis), 11tl (Miroslaw
Trembecki/Corbis); iStockphoto: 6, 8tl, 8b,
9b, 10bl, 13tr, 15tr; Rex Features: 8tr (Henryk
T. Kaiser/Rex Features), 16tl (East News/Rex
Features), 17b (Piotr Drozdzik/Rex Features).